An Active Society in a Networked World

Borut Rončević and Tamara Besednjak Valič

An Active Society in
a Networked World

The Cultural Political Economy of Grand Strategies

**Bibliographic Information published by the
Deutsche Nationalbibliothek**
The Deutsche Nationalbibliothek lists this publication in the Deutsche
Nationalbibliografie; detailed bibliographic data is available online at
http://dnb.d-nb.de.

Library of Congress Cataloging-in-Publication Data
A CIP catalog record for this book has been applied for at the
Library of Congress.

This publication was financially co-funded by the Erasmus+ programme of the
European Union, Key Action: Erasmus+, Jean Monnet, Action Type: Jean Monnet
Chair, Project Reference: 575243-EPP-1-2016-1-SI-EPPJMO-CHAIR.
The European Commission's support for the production of this publication does not
constitute an endorsement of the contents, which reflect the views only of the
authors, and the Commission cannot be held responsible for any use which may be
made of the information contained therein.

The authors also acknowledge the financial support from the Slovenian Research
Agency (research core funding No. P1-0383).

ISBN 978-3-631-88390-7 (Print)
E-ISBN 978-3-631-88394-5 (E-PDF)
E-ISBN 978-3-631-88395-2 (E-PUB)
10.3726/b19930

Contents

Introduction

The subject of this book is the complex and controversial issues of the implementation of the EU's grand strategies, with a particular interest in the developmental success of the newest members of the European Union, the former post-socialist societies. Many post-socialist countries became members of the European Union in a 'big bang' enlargement a decade and a half ago, with the second, smaller enlargements following in 2007 and 2013. They joined after lengthy negotiations and upon meeting a set of criteria with respect to their economic, political, and administrative performances. Furthermore, it was assumed that membership in the EU would further reduce the gap between its old and new members, not least due to a joint strategic approach, embodied in the grand strategies of the European Union, the Lisbon Strategy (2000–2010) and Europe 2020 (2011–2020). However, this may have been an overly ambitious expectation, both towards the EU grand strategies, as well as towards the new Member States.

The European Union implementation deficit has become proverbial failure, a phenomenon that is the subject of intense interest by both researchers and policymakers (Makarovič et al., 2014; Haverland and Romeijn, 2007; Borghetto and Franchino, 2010; Tomšič and Vehovar, 2012). While the impact of Europe 2020 has yet to be researched in greater detail, some work does exist (Stec and Grzebyk, 2018; Makarovič et al., 2014), revealing substantial differences in implementation among the Member States, especially along the divisions between North and West on one hand and East and South on the other (Wüst and Rogge, 2022; Kasprzyk and Wojnar, 2021). A research study based on the Cultural Political Economy approach, based on evolutionary mechanisms of variation, selection, and retention of dominant discourses (Jessop, 2004; Jessop, 2010; Jessop and Oosterlynck, 2008), as well as on mechanisms of selectivities (Ngai-Ling and Jessop, 2014), has concluded that if the EU is to successfully meet its developmental challenges, it is vital to develop more efficient mechanisms of retention of selected discourses (Makarovič et al., 2014: 624).

However, many political, cultural, social, economic and other differences still exist between the so-called old and new EU members, stemming from their different socio-political heritages. One such perceived
trend that illustrates these persisting differences is the alleged hollowing
and backsliding of democracy in East-Central Europe. Greskovits (2015)
defines 'hollowing' as declining popular involvement in democracy, and
'backsliding' as destabilisation and reverting to semi-authoritarian practices, noticing that 'the region's pure neoliberal capitalist regimes are like-
lier to undermine popular political participation than those which try to
balance marketization with relatively generous social protection for its
losers' (Greskovits, 2015: 28). As more specifically explained by Berend
and Bugarič (2015: 770), 'in political terms, democratic consolidation is
still far from complete. Instead, new forms of "illiberal democracy" which
are emerging reveal the vulnerability of "consolidated democracies" such
as Hungary or Slovenia to "democratic regression".' The case of Slovenia
shows that even after three decades of post-socialist transition sentiments
and practices that are incompatible with democratic principles remain very
much alive (Kleindienst and Tomšič, 2017; Kleindienst and Tomšič, 2021,
Prijon and Tomšič, 2021), also in the field of media (Bratina, 2021).[1]

Given these observations, the central focus of our interest is the study
of possibilities and limitations of strategic steering of the economic development in the context of comprehensive societal development, such
as the Europe 2020 intention of achieving 'smart, inclusive and sustainable growth'. This grand strategy was developed with the intent to be
the strategy of the European Union, its Member States and their regions,
implemented through the smart specialisation mechanism (Foray, 2015).
However, is this really the case? Although it would be interesting to consider what the implications are for the current Agenda 2030 and its Strategic Development Goals, and some work on the topic already exists
(Tutak et al., 2021; Szymańska, 2021; Ferran Villa, 2021), we will not
dedicate significant attention to this strategic document.

---

1   This is why some authors stress that the interpretation of human dignity (Klein-
    dienst, 2017, 2019, 2019b) which represents a base of democratic political
    culture, is particularly relevant in the 'new democracies' of East-Central Europe
    (Kleindienst and Tomšič, 2017).

The development of post-socialist countries, their successful and less successful aspects, is well documented. In the mid-1990s, Klaus Nielsen, Bob Jessop, and Jerzy Hausner stated that in the light of so many emerging publications about these problems every author should have a very good reason for additional enlargement of the already expansive corpus of literature (Nielsen et al., 1995: 3). The above-mentioned authors substantiated their contribution by researching dialectics, structure, and strategic action in the processes of post-socialist transformation. They linked the research on the unique process with some general problems of political economy and social theory. Three decades later, we need an even better excuse to engage in our exploration. Our excuse is to tackle the issue of universal and continually emerging problems of strategic steering of complex societies.

Despite the expansive corpus of literature, the issues are far from exhaustively researched and numerous unsolved questions and dilemmas remain. First, can already existing theoretical and methodological approaches be used or at least modified for research on the development of contemporary societies? In the early transitology, different authors mostly emphasised the relationship with developmental studies, which evolved by researching third-world countries and post-communist studies (Bunce, 1998; Karl and Scmitter, 1995; Ma, 1998; Wiarda, 2002). The question of applicability of neoclassical economic theory, which was, because of the influence of some international organisations, generously employed for the formation of recipes for the East-European transition, even though economic science was unable to construct mainstream economic theory capable of explaining the success of transition processes, was also often raised (Bell, 2012). Can the multi-level and more democratic approach of the current EU grand strategies avoid the perils, disappointments, and considerable discrepancies between expectations raised by ideas for post-socialist institutional changes and the consequences of measures that did not take into account specific characteristics of post-socialist societies (Genov, 1999: 58–61, Szelenyi, 2014; Gevorkyan, 2018)?

Second, what is the role of purposeful action in developmental trajectories? Are they the result of strategic choice – if that choice was even possible – or does the path-dependency play the central role (Rončević and Makarovič, 2010; Beyer in Wielghos, 2001)?

Third, in the specific context of Eastern Europe, even after decades of scholarship there is a fundamental disagreement about transition being a story of success or not (Berend and Bugarič, 2015; Shleifer and Treisman, 2014; Poznanski, 2001; Janos, 2001; Burawoy, 2001; Berend, 2001). So, as we can see, this research area still presents numerous challenges and unsolved questions.

Finally, it should be emphasised that processes of post-socialist development represent unique empirical evidence, which enables new insights into some universal issues from the social development area of research; amongst them are the issue of developmental factors and the possibility of constructing efficacious developmental policies.

Besides the above-mentioned issues, the entrance into various supranational organizations (the EU, OECD, etc.) raises some additional issues that should be attempted to be resolved. How does the entrance into the company of higher developed societies influence the developmental performances of these societies? Which strategies should be used in facing these challenges? In this context, the issue of the genesis of systemic competitiveness (Esser et al., 1996) of post-socialist societies and the possibility of its reinforcement is especially relevant.

The dilemma of whether the social development of modern societies should be subjected to planned steering or courses of developmental trajectories should be left to self-regulation (i.e., social evolution) is without doubt one of the most important and the most prominent dilemmas in the history of social and (at the research on the economic system) economic thought. From the reflection of this issue arises the famous remark of Adam Smith (Wealth of Nations, 1776): 'People of the same trade seldom meet together, even for merriment and diversion, but the conversation ends in a conspiracy against the public, or in some contrivance to raise prices'. However, the universality of specific developmental issues does not presuppose the universal validity of solutions to these issues. Analysis of some defined situations and measures, based on this analysis, can be completely irrelevant when implemented in different environments. The problem should be approached with the consideration of the empirical level, which presupposes focusing on structural characteristics of defined social environment and on analysis of conditions that could enable or prevent specific ways of the steering or self-steering of social development.

There is no universal solution to the above-mentioned dilemma, and specific solutions only work in specific societal constellations. This is the reason that attempts for the transplantation of institutional arrangements into incompatible environment usually involve high costs and chronically suboptimal efficacy. One example of such a policy is the overvaluation of the creative potential of chaos in the form of a too-fast liberalisation of the economy, overhasty privatisation, and rash diminishing of the role of the state (Genov, 1999), which led to too high social and economic costs.

Of course, post-socialist societies differed greatly in the rate at which the state relinquished its role in the economy. As pointed out by Szelenyi who emphasised:

> [...] "there are many shades and phases within neo-liberalism: Poland is quite different from Hungary, the Czech Republic from Slovakia. The most unusual case of neo-liberalism is Slovenia – it followed, at least initially, a more gradualist approach, especially in terms of privatization. It opened up to international capital much slower than the other Central European countries, while state owned enterprises were downsized which led to a sharp drop in employment, many firms remained in the possession of their management and workers. Nevertheless, the similarities among the East Central European countries in terms of their transformational trajectory are more pronounced than their differences" (2014: 7).

Successful strategies of sustained[2] development must take into account complicated relationships of co-dependency between various partial systems if they wish to attain long-term success. Long-term and lasting enhancement of economic development is only possible when there is a transition to a higher developmental level, meaning when there are simultaneous changes in various dimensions of development. Without education of the workforce, the improvement of infrastructure and quality of administrative institutions, the long-term enlargement of economic success is not possible. Likewise, the long-term performance of processes of democratisation is not possible without adequate economic and social development. This was also grasped by authors of various studies of competitiveness

---

2   The term 'sustained development' pertains to the development, based on foundations that enable long-term positive trends. The term 'sustainable development' could also be used here. However, sustainable development pertains to the broader concept with a strong ecological connotation, which is less relevant in the context of this book.

(like *World Competitiveness Yearbook* or *The Global Competitiveness Report*), which in their estimation of competitiveness of countries include numerous dimensions.

Consequently, this book is an analysis of strategic steering of economic development. However, it is not an economic study but a classic sociological analysis focused on economic subsystem.

In the book, we rely on relativistic and holistic comprehension of development. Relativism implies the multi-directionality of the processes of modernisation and opposes normativism, meaning the determination of 'necessary' directions of social development. Normativism is one of the key characteristics of older theories of social development (modernisation developmental theories of Rostow or McCleland, by Marxism-influenced theories like for example Frank's underdevelopment theory, Cardoso's dependency theory, modes of production theory) which from the 1950s most significantly marked the research on developmental trajectories of less-developed countries (at the time, these were mostly the countries of the Third World). Exaggerated and unfounded normativism of such comprehension of development became clear not only with the decrease of modernisation euphoria (amongst the reasons for this decrease were also numerous unplanned negative consequences of developmental programmes). In the context of the research on economic development, numerous other empirical trends might be even more important, especially the evidence of the multi-linear nature of capitalist development (which expresses itself in quite numerous new, specific, and usually absolutely original types of industrialisation, for example in Japan, Ireland, Finland, the Little Asian Tigers, etc.). Finally, some more recent theories, especially theories of social capital (see Williams et al., 2021; Westlund and Adam, 2010; Adam and Rončević, 2003) indicate that the presence of specific – conditionally speaking – 'premodern' cultural patterns is necessary for the proper and effective functioning of some of the most notorious artefacts and mechanisms of steering of developmentally successful 'modern' societies (primarily working market economy and parliamentary democracy).

In searching for the solutions to the above-mentioned issues, we will rely on some more sophisticated conceptualisations, which upgrade simplified comprehension of hierarchical strategic processes and developmental policies used by the state to stimulate development with direct interventions.

We will focus on the possibilities of more subtle modes of intervention into the border conditions of action (contextual intervention) and various negotiation or discursive forms of strategic processes. Contextual intervention is the only type of intervention that is based on hierarchical constellations and that considers the autonomy of partial systems. It is a way of intervention that does not interfere with partial systems themselves but encroaches on border conditions of their actions (e.g., reduction of prices by encouraging competition and not by mechanisms of price regulation). Systemic discourse is a process during which there is communication between actors within the framework of various negotiation systems, networks, and similar (Willke, 1993).

In our study, much attention will be paid to this type of social steering and to preconditions for such approach. The process of creation of strategies and level of socio-cultural suppositions of innovative forms of dialogue in heterarchical network interactions between enterprises, research, and development organisations, government and intermediary institutions will be of special interest. After all, the ability of the state to participate in the constructive interaction with other potentially relevant actors and the ability to produce impulses for stimulation of cooperation depends on this.

We will also have to resolve the issue of specific nature and developmental dynamics of post-socialist societies. Extensive empirical evidence unequivocally attests to the amazing differences in the developmental success of transitional societies (see, e.g., Gevorkyan, 2018). Some authors describe reestablishment of new, multi-pole arrangement on the territory of post-socialist Europe. This means that individual countries face very different developmental problems and developmental goals, which are (independently of the often unrealistic programme and strategic documents), in fact, incomparable. Moreover these countries face the problems of modernisation in very different ways.

In the context of the debate, we will have to resolve the following issue: are post-socialist societies, in fact, modern societies with high degrees of functional differentiation? In the light of the decades-long constant penetration of political system into other partial systems, one can pose a question: is a political system after a relatively short period (considering Dahrendorf's warning about excessively optimistic expectations about the end of transition) capable of taking into account specific logics of action of partial systems or does it still exploit that potentials of hierarchical steering and in accordance with its own systemic logic of influence penetrates directly into the systems itself, using, of course, more sophisticated mechanisms than in the past? This can manifest in various ways, for example, by a large share of prices still controlled by the state or by the high shares of state ownership and interference in the business policies of enterprises, which is not in accordance with economic logic. If this is the case, we can face two potential consequences. It can come to the ignorance of those interventions of the political system that are not perceived as being relevant by economy – this is a wasteful usage of state resources. Or the abuse of political power can lead to the processes of regressive dedifferentiation of functionally differentiated societies. I think that in the case of post-socialist societies both possibilities are quite real and deserve our attention.

There are two central hypotheses. First, in the context of post-socialist societies of Central and Eastern Europe, strategic steering of social development is possible if it follows heterarchical principles of contextual intervention and systemic discourse. Second, qualities of socio-cultural field and technocratic competence are key resources for solving the problems of trust, cooperation, and articulation of interests that arise in such strategic steering.

The first chapter is an overview of theoretical foundations for the analysis, focused on steering of economic development in the context of modern societies, which are characterised by the primacy of functional differentiation and growing complexity. Emphasis will be laid on the (in) ability of hierarchical formation of developmental strategies and the potential role of the state in this process. We will more particularly lean on the systems theory of Niklas Luhmann and Helmut Willke but will simultaneously expose some limitations of these approaches, especially the difficulty of grasping more complex forms of strategic processes that are taking place in communications within the network of individual or collective actors. While social systems theory has developed into a relevant macrosocial theory, some doubts remain about some more specific applications (Šubrt, 2020). Socio-cultural suppositions of successful strategic steering also cannot be successfully explained by systems theory.

Research into intentional strategic steering is mostly undertaken by experts in the fields of management and theory of organisation. The second chapter focuses on the concept of strategic steering of social development in the context of Innovation 2.0 and the possibilities of such approach. Here, the strategic process is understood as a social process taking place in a special field between individual and collective actors and emergent social structures.

The third chapter focuses on the Cultural Political Economy of the EU grand strategies. Emphasis will be laid on the Lisbon Strategy and Europe 2020, since the most recent document Agenda 2030 and its Sustainable Development Goals are at an early stage of implementation. We will study various definitions, research strategies, and the role of social capital in the formation of multi-functional linkages and social learning.

Despite our study being a sociological analysis, we proceed from the supposition that it is necessary to interlink findings made in the framework of various content and disciplinary approaches. Here one should mention newer trends in the epistemological orientation of scientific research like post-normal or post-academic science or the Mode 2 production of knowledge. In these trends, there is a prominent emphasis on teamwork, cooperation between various disciplines, and between researchers and customers, which presupposes some flexibility of research process. New knowledge is produced on the basis of the recombination and reconfiguration of competences, by which it caters to more sophisticated needs (Gibbons, 1996). Mode 2 is thus viewed as a 'transdisciplinary, heterogeneous and hierarchical method that achieves quality through social accountability and reflexivity, leading to results that are highly contextualized' (van Hemert et al., 2009: 444). Mode 2 claims have received mixed reactions (van Hemert et al., 2009; Hessels and van Lente, 2008); however, the essential idea of transdisciplinarity is gaining more and more support as it is becoming increasingly clear that the highly interrelated, cross-cutting, complex issues of modern societies require more complex, holistic research practices (Rek et al., 2017). Developing and applying sustainable long-term strategies for socio-technical change on the basis of socially robust knowledge seems inevitable (Gudowsky and Peissl, 2016: 1) and it is precisely the transdisciplinary research that is often promoted as a mode of knowledge production that is effective in addressing and solving current sustainability challenges (Golob and Makarovič, 2021; Džajić Uršič, 2019, Besednjak Valič and Džajić Uršič, 2021). Its effectiveness stems from its closeness to practice-based/situated expertise and real-life problem contexts (Polk, 2015: 110).

While none of the emerging approaches to new knowledge production remains uncontested, it is safe to say that strict separation between various approaches is *passé*; which is expressed in various ways in the frame of this study. One example of this is approaching the research on the issue of economic development, which was for a long time in the domain of economic science, with sociological methods. In this way, existing studies can be enriched with new insights, which especially means the incorporation of some factors that were, up until now, given (too) little consideration to (culture, social structure) or their revaluation (negative attitude toward the role of social relations). Our study is thus not installed within the frame of individual theoretic tradition; it draws, as necessary, from a rich set of sociological theories – systems theory, network theory, neo-institutional analysis, social becoming approach – and uses the findings of various disciplines and sub-disciplines.

The EU, grand strategies, and policy-making: Theoretical foundations

The EU has been attempting to uplift its global position by implementing so-called grand strategies. The aim of these strategies was to increase its competitiveness (see more in Makarovič et. al., 2014). However, since the first comprehensive attempt, the Lisbon Strategy, the EU has been experiencing the consequences of an implementation deficit (ibid, also Rončević, 2019). Following the aims of the now past EU grand strategy – Europe 2020 – it provides numerous guidelines on how to address and meet the needs for successful, smart, and inclusive growth. For the EU to be able to achieve the ambitious goals set up in its grand strategy, retention and reinforcement mechanisms must be put in place. By doing so, all engaged stakeholders can identify the co-ownership of the proposed strategy contributing to its successful implementation. Because cultural foundations play an important part in the process and its success (see more in Kleindienst and Tomšič, 2017; Kleindienst and Tomšič, 2018), a further analysis of the relationship between the institutional system and the cultural platform is necessary. To be able to provide for that, a robust sociological conceptual model is requested, to customise both the operationalisation and research methodology.

Having said that, the theoretical foundations for dealing with the role of the state and other actors such as the European Union in the steering of social development should be laid. In the frame of various disciplines, numerous approaches have been developed for dealing with this issue. Building of these foundations is not a goal *per se*, it is *conditio sine qua non* for the analysis of developmental processes, despite these themes having, in the last instance, applicative potentials: 'Theories shape researchers' thinking processes, lay the foundation for their analytical framework, guide their research theses, and set their research agendas. In addition, theories lead researchers to adopt certain methodologies, attract them to examine certain data sets, and influence them to draw certain conclusions and policy implications' (So, 1990: 11).

While we will engage numerous theoretical approaches that are not within the frame of the same tradition, and some are not even dealing with the same level of analysis, the beginning of this chapter will nevertheless be dedicated to the study of approaches to the issue of steering that are in the framework of sociological systems theory as developed by Niklas Luhmann and by his interpreters and critics, especially Helmut Willke. Sociological systems theory[3] is very well suited for the purposes of our study and for dealing with steering mechanisms of (post)modern societies. Luhmann's theory with its offshoots is the last theory that became part of the big macro-sociological theories (so-called 'grand theories')[4]. This has important consequences. First, it has to be emphasised that despite Luhmann's stressing his intention not being the search for new insights on the basis of exegesis of sociological classics but the integration of discoveries of interdisciplinary studies (incorporation of concepts from the field of research on bio-organisms could be included here) his work represents an upgrade or modification of existing approaches, at least to some degree. In that regard, numerous points of contact between Luhmann's and Parsons' systems theory can be particularly highlighted (Leydesdorff, 2010). Relation to older and alternative conceptualisations of the role of the state can thus be established based on Luhmann's systems theory. At the same time, it can serve as a good foundation for analysis of actual trends in the field of research on steering, especially various approaches within the frame of the theory of networks (Messner, 2013; van Assche et al., 2011; Castells, 1997).

---

3   There are numerous variations of systems theory; they can be found in various sciences as well as in various specialisations in the framework of social and political sciences. When talking about sociological systems theory, I describe the theoretical opus of Niklas Luhmann as well as a more sophisticated upgrade of his implementations, done by Helmut Willke. The only exceptions to that are those parts of the text where it can be clearly seen from the context that I am talking about Luhmann's work.

4   Two other similar attempts from the period of Luhmann's creative opus should also be mentioned here. The first is Habermas' work *Theorie des Kommunikativen Handelns* (Habermas, 1981). The second is Giddens' analysis in the framework of many studies, especially *The Constitution of Society* (1984) where he presented theory of structuration.

The concept of system differentiation can also be applied in the context of European Union studies, although it was not developed for this purpose. It describes the establishment of partial systems within the frames of existing systems and enables the analysis of relations between collective actors, situated on different levels. It is not an attempt at integration of micro-macro or agent-structure (see Ritzer and Goodman, 2003), but communication between actors, situated on different levels, is important for the comprehension of concrete strategic practices. Particularly in research on the steering of economic development and the creation of strategic orientations, dialogue and interpenetration between various levels usually do occur. The model for analysis of systemic competitiveness, developed by Esser and co-authors, thus incorporates no less than four levels: micro, mezzo, macro, and meta (Esser et al., 1996). When researching the economy, it is not hard to imagine functional differentiation. The existence of economy as an independent social sub-system – insofar as it fulfils this criterion – itself is a result of functional differentiation in the process of modernisation. We must deal with differentiation also in the frame of economy, which further differentiates itself into various branches, for example. On the micro-level, partial sub-systems developed in the form of various specialised departments in larger enterprises, each of them fulfilling its own role (purchase, production, marketing, staff management, public relations, etc.). Examples of this are business clusters, where it comes to a linkage between flexible and *specialized* enterprises, performing at a particular level in the process of creation of new value (more on this in the third chapter).

The issue of steering of economic development, as it is outlined in the present study, is not merely a narrow technological issue; instead, it is connected with broader questions of developmental trajectories, social evolution, and relations between social sub-systems, despite our decision not to stay at the macro level of empirical analysis. Systems theory is macro theory, and this is why it is at this point more appropriate than numerous mezzo theories about the role of the state, for example, public-private partnership (Mugarura, 2020; Kouwenhoven, 1993), neo-etatism, competitive state, or neo-statism (McNally, 2019; Weiss and Hobson, 1995), minimal state (Nozick, 1974) etc. This is a complex issue, and one needs a complex categorical apparatus in order to be able to explain it. In this regard, systems theory is a universal theory. This universality reveals itself in three aspects (Willke, 1993a: 1–4). First, it does not focus on research of a particular area or aspect of sociological thought; instead, it attempts to provide a frame within which one can search for answers to all questions (*fachspezifische Universalität*). Second, general systems theory as an interdisciplinary science was developed on the basis of the astounding similarity of system problems, arising within the frame of various sciences. Sociological systems theory can thus be regarded as part of the universal heuristic programme (*interdisziplinäre Universalität*).[5] Third, social relations in modern societies are complex and cannot be reduced to simple categories (*Universalität des Problems der Kompleksität*). When analysing complex problems, such as those we examine in the European Union studies, sociological systems theory thus represents an adequate pillar despite numerous critiques of its (too) comprehensive conceptual apparatus, (too) numerous thought experiments, and innovations that are sometimes an end in themselves[6].

It should be particularly emphasised that systems theory dealt exhaustively with issues of mechanisms of steering of development (possibilities and limitations of evolutionary/market and hierarchical principles) and the role of the state or political system. Within the frame of discussions about individual sub-systems, one can also pose a question about relations between economy, state, and workforce within the frame of neo-corporatist discursive mechanisms, or – at the mezzo level – about the establishment of communication between various actors that participate in forming business clusters. In some more refined forms, it came to innovative attempts of upgrading classical mechanisms for self-steering of modern societies (at the concept of contextual intervention) and to conceptualisation of new mechanisms (system discourse) (Willke, 1993). Some authors showed that

---

5   Some authors criticize this aspect of Luhmann's systems theory. One typical case is the concept of autopoiesis; Luhmann took this concept from Maturana and Varela, who used it in the research of bio-organisms. Maturana and Varela insisted that social systems are not autopoietic (Cadenas and Marcelo, 2015).

6   This critique occurs mostly for Luhmann's version of systems theory, which is at the same time among the most influential ones.

sociological systems theory can be used for the analysis of strategic processes in the frames of organisations (Seidl and Mormann, 2015).

Luhmann's systems theory and its concepts' role in explaining issues of
communist societies and post-communist transition (Adam et al., 2005;
Bernik and Rončević, 2002) is not an unimportant one. Its explanatory
power was particularly proved in the analysis of changing functions of a
political sub-system in ex-socialist societies and in the analysis of changes
in relation to the political system in regard to other sub-systems, in our
case, in regard to the economy.

The state as the central point of society: Early approaches

Modern debates about mechanisms of social steering and the role of the
state in the formation of developmental measures did not come into being
in a vacuum: they originate from a rich tradition. To better understand
the content and the consequences of conclusions reached by authors in the
frame of systems theory, it is necessary to be familiar with the theoretical
context within which it developed. To this end, we will review those basic
aspects of various theories of steering that are relevant in the context of
the present study.

These discussions were mainly evolving around – if we simplify slightly –
the dilemma of whether the coordination of society should be reached by
using mechanisms of hierarchical intervention or if it should be a spontaneous evolutionary process. Or, if we use a more known contrariety,
they were evolving around disputation about the state versus the market.
As was shown by the progress in the area of research on social coordination and steering, this dilemma has been exceeded for some time now.
This is borne out by more sophisticated approaches that remain within
the frames of these discussions; here the following should be particularly
emphasised: the work of Helmut Willke (1993), the conceptualisation of
new ways of social (self)steering (reflexion, contextual intervention and
systemic discourse) – as well as by literature dealing with the research on
network forms of coordination.

The first theories of social steering regarded hierarchy as key or even
as the sole mechanism and by this they made a long-term mark on the
trends in the area of research on social steering. These theories evolved on

the basis of regarding the state as a unified, hierarchically superior, and sovereign centre of decision-making. This approach can also be found in the work of Max Weber, who defined the state as an entity that claims a monopoly on the legitimate use of violence. From this period is also the conceptualisation of state as an entity that steers social development using two mechanisms: law and power. The state was described as the top of the social pyramid, as 'nervous centre of the organism that regulates public affairs...' (Messner, 2013: 47). Despite the distinction between the state and civil society, which was made by Hegel, the state is not limited to exercising only external sovereignty. Fundamental assumptions of internal sovereignty are the separation of state and civil society (systems theory would call it systemic differentiation) and the supposition of hierarchical superiority of the state over the 'civil society'. Hegel defines civil society as a stage of difference that intervenes between the family and the state. This is the reason that the concept of civil society in the period after 'the great transformation' (Polany, 2001), when economic activities moved out of the framework of all-embracing family into the framework of specialised subsystems, also embracing economic systems. It follows from this that the sovereignty of the state also holds good for the economy.

Numerous later theories could not liberate themselves from the 'state-centred' paradigm either. Even some theories that are quite close to economic liberalism could also be placed amongst them. Messner (2013) places pluralism amongst them. This approach regards the state as a centre of society, formulating and executing binding decisions. It focuses especially on researching mechanisms of parliamentary democracy, within the frames of which interactions between various interests take place. They transform themselves into political power or incorporate themselves into processes of influencing the bearers of political power. Despite the state being the core of society, this fact *per se* does not presuppose hierarchical principles of steering. In the framework of state institutions (parliament) runs competition that leads, as it is also valid for market mechanisms, to the establishment of equilibrium. In the frame of pluralistic theories, the majority of attention is focused on politics dimension of policy, while polity remains the black box, from which we can observe only input and output. Policy dimension, so important for research on steering (in the context of this study, in the research on politics for stimulation of economic development) is dismissed with the assumption that output (for example concrete programmes and measures) is a manifestation of equilibrium. For that reason, this part of analysis is neglected.

Schumpeter (1934) corrected this simplified theory in the frame of his concept of elitist democracy, but he too interprets the state as the centre of social decision-making. Still, the inclusion of polity dimension can be noted within the frame of his approach. Schumpeter describes a political process, unrolling in the context in which the state is alienated from society, as a process of competition between elites. Equilibrium is thus not determined by equal competition between all interested actors; it is determined by the elitist state. Because other actors cannot articulate the need, the state is the one that must be able to detect problems when they are still in the early stage.

In the first decades following the Second World War, the key theoretical orientation, falling within the frames of the state-centric paradigm, was Keynesianism, which in practice manifested itself in the form of the welfare state and 'planned' capitalism. Contrary to pluralistic approaches, it interprets the role of the state as the centre of society in a positive way. The growing range of activities of the state caused a growing interest in the polity dimension, for the institutional framework, specifically for political-administrative institutions in the frame of which politics and policy are unrolling. This vision rests on three pillars (Messner, 2013: 56):

1. Some premises from the theory of democracy – harmonistic ideas about processes of decision-making and equilibrium of interests that originate from pluralism (politics dimension);
2. Interventionist and welfare-oriented state apparatus (polity dimension), which was able to construct a system of social security (policy dimension);
3. On the level of economic politics, an important role is played by orientation toward the limitation of instabilities of capitalist development and the creation of preconditions for social justice and equal opportunities.

In this framework, the state was responsible for the stimulation of economic efficacy and socially balanced development, which was achieved by the use of economic politics (particularly by the use of macroeconomic instruments and stimulation of demand) and by the use of restrictive measures for the purpose of social transfers.

In this sense, legitimacy of the state and suchlike arrangements depends on the success of the economy (capacity to generate resources for redistribution) and on the loyalty of social actors. This model was prevalent until the beginning of the 1970s, when Keynesian macroeconomic management was no longer able to provide high levels of economic growth and full employment.

The rather predictable and stable environment, which was in part the result of international financial arrangements (Bretton Woods) and the externalisation of costs (low prices of oil) became more dynamic and less predictable. This slowly led to the awareness about limitations of such an approach.

Partial decentralisation: Neo-corporatism

Rising social corporatism (Schmitter, 1979) or neo-corporatism in the middle of the 1970s and 1980s (Lehmbruch, 1979; Katzenstein, 1985) represents an important alternative to the pluralistic and Keynesian comprehension of the state as the centre of society and with that to the sphere in which confrontation and communication between various interests are taking place. In contrast to competition and confrontation as a way toward the equilibrium, neo-corporatism emphasises the positive effects of cooperation, political stability, and the achievement of compromises. Attention is, contrary to the principles of the state's hierarchical steering, paid to the voluntary communication between actors.

Katzenstein analysed neo-corporatist arrangements that were established in seven small European countries in the period after the Second World War. Regardless of their form, be it liberal (Netherlands, Belgium, Switzerland) or social neo-corporatism (Austria, Sweden, Denmark, Norwegian), there are three characteristics typical of this system. The first characteristic is the ideology of social partnership in solving issues of economic and social politics that permeates everyday politics and eases social conflicts between employers and trade unions. It does not mean that there are no unresolved issues. On the contrary, many dilemmas and disputes exist in society, but it is important that these conflicts are continually being solved in the frame of negotiating mechanisms in the frame of an inexactly determined but solid general consensus about the public interest. One could also call it the 'developmental consensus'. The second characteristic is a rather centralised system of interest groups that ensures the control of lower levels and obedience to resolutions that were adopted on the highest level. This also ensures greater inclusion (of employees and employers). The third characteristic is voluntary (and informal) coordination of conflicting goals in the processes of ongoing negotiation between interest groups, state and political parties (Katzenstein, 1985).

Neo-corporatism thus does not represent a complete alternative or paradigmatic shift in the true sense of the word. It would be more accurate to say that it attempts to upgrade some of the previous approaches. This approach also did not relinquish the concept of hierarchical steering, and this is one of its important characteristics. On the one hand, it does not accept clear functional differentiation between the state and other partial systems; on the other hand, it rejects the simplified logic about competition between them (Messner, 2013: 71). In pluralism, the state is the centre of society (and is influenced by various pressure groups) and polyarchy and competition exist between interest groups. In neo-corporatism, more or less equal communication exists between systems that do not compete with each other, are internally strongly centralised, and are hierarchically regulated. In this sense, other actors are not separated or isolated from the political process but are integrated into it.

The majority of authors analyse neo-corporatist arrangements as an instrument for the coordination of economic politics. Moreover, Katzenstein's analysis of corporatism is a study of adapting strategies of small countries that are forced into opening to the international environment. Neo-corporatist discussions are important because they provided new insights into relations between various politics and showed the complexity and interdependence of various aspects of development, specifically the dependence of economic development from other dimensions, in this case especially from social dimension and consensus.

However, while neo-corporatism provided some new insights into the problems of steering, it also has numerous weak points. The most important criticism comes from the above-mentioned fact that neo-corporatism over-emphasised the principle of hierarchy in social steering and that it limited itself to the research on relations in the triad of state-employers-trade unions. By following the principle of hierarchical relations in the internal structure of each of the three partners, neo-corporatism was supposed to enable a high degree of inclusion and solve the problems pertaining to implementation of developmental policies. However, excessive concentration on the above-mentioned three partners led to other potentially relevant actors being left out of the analysis and process of decision-making. With that, the Keynesians headed mostly for research on centripetal forces and the issue of redistribution (Messner, 2013: 76) and missed two issues. First, numerous centrifugal forces exist in society. In the context of societies in which there is no 'culture of conflict', it can come to paralysis of communication, or, such relations can lead to the promotion of particularistic interest, patron-client relationships, and endless compromises, which also paralyse the developmental potentials of developed societies. Examples of this are some rigid welfare states in some socio-democratic countries, such as Germany (Esping-Andersen, 1996). Second, if communication is focused on the question of redistribution, this can lead to problems in those politics where the production of resources that cannot be produced by classical redistribution mechanisms needs to be done. Highly developed and complex societies do not compete on the basis of natural resources, cheap labour force, and other 'fundamental factors' (Porter, 1990), but systemic competitiveness (Esser et al., 1996) and developmental performances (Adam et al., 2005a) depend on numerous intangible factors.

Certainly, one important positive contribution of studies of neo-corporatism is that they show how the issue of steering is not just an issue of technocratic capacities of the state; instead, it is a broader issue that could be labelled as 'self-steering capacities of society'. This is the reason that steering in the conditions of growing complexity is not just a technocratic problem that could be solved by growing investment into the capacities of state apparatus.

Inability of steering: Economy as complex system

Complexity, nonlinearity, chaos in economy

Paul Ormerod stated that modern orthodox economic science (here he refers to neoclassical analysis) is in the methodological and epistemological sense isolated from its roots in 18th and 19th centuries, when classic scholars like Malthus, Smith, Ricardo or Marx were not afraid to theorize but used this theory to describe reality. In contrast to this, in research on the action of market mechanism of self-steering, there are so many unrealistic, simplified assumptions[7] integrated into sophisticated econometric models that it seems that a professional culture that exalts 'esoteric irrelevance' (Ormerod, 1994) has developed in the frame of the economy. The assumption of perfectly rational agents produces elegant economic science, but it is 'restrictive and often unrealistic' (Arthur, 2021: 136). Hence the development of complexity economics, which relaxed these assumptions. Agents differ, have imperfect information, sometimes even unclear goals, which must change as they try to make sense of the situation (Ibid.), for example, in the case of a mutually supported, well-implemented strategic shift to green economy, as promoted by Europe 2020 and now Agenda 2030, and changing customer behaviour rewarding this shift.

Disregarding complex reality can also be found in theories of steering and forming of policies that are based on suppositions about the possibility of successful rational steering of economic development in modern societies. Multi-layered problems of self-steering capacities are thus reduced to the level of technocratic problem. Strategic steering in line with Simon's synoptic rational model of comprehensive planning would only be possible if some presumptions would hold true. These presumptions were exposed, for example by Ernst-Hasso Ritter. First, the environment is structured in a rather simple way. Second, politics and measures implemented by the state influence the environment in accordance with rather simple causal relationships. Third, similarly as in the construction of models of

---

7   In 1968 mathematical economist Roy Radner proved the existence of competitive equilibrium. However, Radner also showed that in order for his proof to be valid, every economic actor should possess complete information and limitless calculating abilities (Ormerod, 1994: 89–90).

market action, there is an assumption of complete information available to the actors of planning (i.e., the state). Fourth, goals defined by the central actor must also be unconditionally accepted by other actors (Ritter in Messner, 2013: 59). Helmut Willke likewise indicated three fundamental suppositions of theories of rational steering that are problematic because of the complexity of the environment. First, goals and priorities, as well as means, resources, and instruments needed to obtain these goals, have to be clearly defined, together with clear causal relationships. Second, criteria for goal attainment, such as profitability, effectiveness, and efficacy, have to be clearly defined. Third, the basic presumption is that individual actors will aggregate their behaviour in rational action with optimal effect (Willke, 1992: 114).

However, empirical evidence clearly indicates that these suppositions are not valid. Numerous studies have recognised the complexity of developmental trajectories. On the level of broader social development, an excellent example of this is presented by the study of David Landes (1999) about the rising and falling of great empires, which attempts to embrace numerous complex interdependencies of factors, specific for individual empires (each has its own story). A study of European industrialization in the 19th century, made by Berend and Ranki (1982) or early research on great differences in the development of each of the four Asian Tigers (Kim and Nelson, 2000; O'Hearn, 1998; Castells, 1998) or research on the Asian Drivers, whose economies embody markedly different combinations of state and capitalist development compared with the industrialised world (Kaplinsky and Messner, 2008: 5) can also be classified as such. Modern societies are complex societies, and developmental processes are complex processes. Dunford and Liu (2017) argue that the crisis of neoliberal globalisation, the progressive slowdown of the economies of the North and of Japan that led global economic growth up to the 1970s, the end of the third wave of multiparty representative democracy, the rise of new powers with distinctive social models and the erosion of a unipolar world and Western global leadership are a set of interconnected trends, which are fundamentally changing the macro-geographies. According to them, these macro-geographies are consequences of uneven and combined development and the analysis of these processes

[...]should draw on a twofold conception of the evolving global system as (1) a set of processes of capital accumulation, unfolding at a variety of scales and (2) an assemblage/constellation of interacting and asymmetrically integrated/interconnected national institutional configurations and interests that shape economic trends and can result in "tectonic spatial shifts". These economic, political and cultural drivers are associated with specific mechanisms of differentiation and equalization of the conditions of production, distribution, consumption and exchange, whose relative weight and character shape comparative development. In capitalist societies enterprises/institutions/countries that are less developed are pressured and able to appropriate technical and social gains from the more advanced. These gains are combined with existing conditions, jumping over intermediate steps, yet generating new contradictions. Outcomes depend on institutional/governance capacities and the degree of support from/ability to resist more advanced rivals. Outcomes involve an unfolding combination/articulation of different stages of development/modes of production and differentiated historical pathways to modernization' (Dunford and Liu, 2017: 4–5).

Luhmann calls an interconnected collection of elements 'complex' when, 'because of immanent constraints in the elements' connective capacity, it is no longer possible at any moment to connect every element with every other element' (Luhmann, 1995: 24). Considering this definition, the economy is, without doubt, a complex system, because all actors that meet among themselves in supply and demand on the market cannot be simultaneously linked to one another but are selecting between relevant units. However, here I am also interested in another aspect connected to all this. The great number of actors and the emergent nature of social phenomena, whose nature is not equal to the linear sum of actions of individuals (the so-called emergence thesis) result in the establishment of difficult-to determine causal relationships, which cannot be reduced to the frames of linear models. In this sense, complex systems can be regarded as systems in which nonlinear, contextually specific, and chaotic trends are taking place.

Research on the complexity of economy strongly attached itself to chaos theory. It should be emphasized that the term 'chaos' in the context of this theory carries a specific meaning that is different from its meaning in everyday use. Walter Buckley describes a chaotic system as a system in which all elements are so weakly linked that there is an equal chance of any element linking with any other element (Buckley, 1998). However, it has to be emphasised that in chaos theory 'chaotic' does not equal 'erratic', and if an individual social system is described as 'chaotic' it does not mean that this system is falling into pieces or is uncontrollable. Chaos is an entangled mixture of order and disorder, regularity and irregularity. There are patterns of behaviour that are irregular but still recognisable as broader categories of behaviour within the frame of which unlimited individual variability exists. Contrary to the theories that assume the formation of equilibrium, chaotic systems are mixtures of stability and instability. This was also noted by Willke: 'In the background of the question about conditions of possibilities of social order [...] is not an interest in order, but the assumption about the normality of chaos. Order represents itself as an improbable state which can be reached under special conditions' (Willke, 1997: 22). However, both Buckley (1998) and Willke concluded that social systems nevertheless time and time again surprise us with their self-preserving capabilities. 'It is obvious that all social systems, including societies, manage to establish robust order again and again' (Willke, 1993: 23).

The issue of social systems as chaotic systems is thus essentially connected to the issue of social order. This social order – the state of equilibrium – can crumble any time, but it also always re-establishes itself. There is a perpetual alternation between order and chaos, which originates from the fact that '[the] condition of its stabilization is at the same time condition of its peril; specific level of complexity that enables order at the same time undermines it' (Ibid: 23). This conclusion was also reached by Stacey in his study of management in chaotic systems: 'When nonlinear systems are pushed from equilibrium into chaos, they are able to spontaneously produce unpredictable, more complex forms of behaviour in the process of self-organization' (Stacey, 1996: 36). More complex forms of behaviour and more complex social structures are thus the answer to growing complexity.

Of course, here we need to ask if empirical evidence confirms the statement that economy as a social system is also a complex (i.e., nonlinear and chaotic) system. Stacey poses a question: why would economic systems, characterised by numerous feedback loops, be an exception in regard to the complexity that was discovered in other spheres of life (Stacey, 1996: 19). Brock and co-authors are of the opinion that for the discovery of chaos by the use of statistical methods one would need data, polluted by stochastic factors, which is rare. At this, they also emphasise that traditional statistical methods are more appropriate for the analysis of trivial systems and less so for chaotic systems (Brock et al., 1991).

Despite that, in literature we can find evidence about the nonlinear and the chaotic nature of economic processes. Let me first bring forward two examples of nonlinear linkages that can have important implications for developmental strategies. In the first case, it is about an issue that is still relevant also in the context of numerous post-socialist societies: the influence of economic reforms on economic growth. On the basis of empirical data, De Melo and Gelb (1996) discovered that in countries where very limited economic reforms were implemented (in the direction of liberalisation of economy), further smaller steps have a negative influence on economic growth. The influence of economic reforms on economic growth became positive only after a specific threshold was reached.

Despite the mentioned problems with data, some proofs of chaotic behaviour in economy do exist. A typical case is represented by Phillips' curve about the correlation of inflation and the rate of unemployment. It says that a negative correlation exists between those two phenomena: with a growing rate of inflation comes the falling of unemployment, and vice versa.

Ormerod analysed data about the correlation between unemployment and inflation in the USA in the period of 1953–1992 (Ormerod, 1994: 129–132). At first glance, it seems that there is no assumed correlation between both phenomena. Formal statistical methods even verify a positive correlation. However, when he sorted data in numerous groups, it turned out that Phillips' curve does exist. It did not show in the quick overview of data because three, perhaps even five various Phillips' curves existed in the mentioned period (it depended on the criteria that were used). This can be explained by the theory of chaos or the explanatory apparatus of the theory of dissipative structures. When a system is influenced by external energy, the state of equilibrium crumbles, but this does not mean the collapse of the system. The state of equilibrium or state of order establishes itself in a new form, at new coordinates. A possible range of coordinates is limited by so-called strange attractors. Because an individual curve does not support only successive years in the analysed period there were even more such shifts or 'collapses of order' than Phillips' curves discovered.

Steering of nonlinear/chaotic systems

The steering of chaotic systems differs greatly from the steering of trivial systems. In trivial systems, every cause has only one single consequence, which means that designers of measures deal only with additive effects, even in the case of the combined effect of various causes. In this case, we are not dealing with the phenomenon of emergence and such (linear) systems can be understood with the help of analysis of individual components. The whole does not exceed the sum of its individual parts. The steering of trivial systems is based on the supposition of negative feedback loop, in which strategic actors attempt to stimulate specific states or trends with measures or a series of measures. They control the results with the help of various mechanisms (system of monitoring) with which they measure the discrepancy between the current and the desired state. On the basis of this discrepancy, they form new measures. They repeat the procedure until they manage to establish the desired state.

However, in nonlinear systems, one single cause can have a great number of consequences; and minimal differences in variation of factor or in variation of state of the system can have unforeseen consequences. In contrast to trivial systems, nonlinear systems have emergent characteristics. A system is more than just the sum of its parts. It means it is difficult to research it by using the analysis of individual parts of the system. A holistic approach is needed. Because of the nature of the system, it is difficult to foresee and measure potential consequences; therefore, steering in nonlinear systems is completely different from steering in trivial systems. A hierarchical approach to steering in chaotic systems is not possible or does not bring desired outcomes, because there are no expected negative feedback loops leading to equilibrium or social order. Chaotic environments require different approaches to the formation of strategies. These systems are characterised by positive feedback loopholes, acting in the opposite way. Instead of decreasing differences between current and desired states, feedback loopholes in the form of various measures continue to increase these differences. Positive feedback loopholes are not just theoretical possibilities or the result of laboratory experiments. Phenomena such as the bandwagon effect, self-fulfilling and self-negating prophecies, chain reactions, vicious and virtuous circles among others, bear witness to that.

This will be discussed in greater detail in the subchapter about measures for strengthening social capital.

Planning in nonlinear systems is also problematic because measures in ideal planning should take into account all possible relevant combinations of causal relations. If a small error occurs in planning, it can happen – or not – that mechanisms of positive feedback loops magnify this error. In this case, the system starts to behave in an unpredictable way, and strategies and measures have unplanned consequences. Numerous cases of developmental strategies, implemented in countries of the Third World and in some traditional communities by international developmental institutions, where consequences were exactly opposite of what was expected, bear witness to the fact that such a possibility is not a completely negligible one. It resulted in unplanned consequences in the form of the disintegration of traditional relations of solidarity that had enabled the survival of the community (Torsvik, 2000). A planner, like any actor on the market, needs to have the ability to determine the optimal strategy in order for rational decision-making; this ability is limited by his information and calculating capacities. Complete information about complex causal relations does not suffice. The planner must also have complete information about future environments and the behaviour of other actors. As shown in the previous subchapter, the economy is a nonlinear system. This also applies to business organisations. This fact has important consequences for the theory and practice of steering of economic development. Possibilities for rational, hierarchical, long-term planning are severely limited. Instead, it is more likely that those processes of self-organisation that enable the formation of structures, which increase the adaptability of the system to changes in the environment and in the systems itself, will be more successful.

According to Stacey (1996: 17), there are two options. The first is to stabilise an enterprise or economy by limiting it with rules, regulations, and plans, which results in stagnation. The alternative option is to free the enterprise or the economy so that it can rely on self-organising interactions, learning and market processes, which provides the possibility for creativity. However, these processes cannot be interpreted only using the conventional distinction between the state or hierarchy versus the market, as it was done by Stacey. It is about the establishment of a new organizational type of 'networks of autonomous actors' (Zeleny, 1997: 251).

It does not mean that the state no longer plays any role in the steering of development: it means that the state cannot achieve this via conventional mechanisms of hierarchical intervention. Its role and mode of action need to change. Answers to the question of possible modes of action in the framework of nonlinear systems can be searched for in an example of small and medium enterprise networks as a form of organisationally open and structurally closed nonlinear autopoietic and self-organising systems. This system must be embedded into an environment that is more complex than small and medium enterprise networks. This environment influences the system, and the system is open to its environment. Moreover, it is in the constant process of 'structural' coupling and, as such, is adaptable. Its survival is enabled by organisational autonomy as well as by structural attachment to ever-changing and chaotic environments (Zeleny, 2001). In contrast, organisationally open and structurally closed systems, which include hierarchies, command systems, and similar, are not capable of structural adaptation to environment. In complex environments, such systems operate sub-optimally, because they are structurally rigid and incapable of adapting.

Adaptation of a system that is not structurally linked to its environment depends on 'symbolic or interpretational information feedback' (Zeleny, 2001: 203), which usually represents the only communication channel with the environment. Without this channel, system would act as a foreign body in environment. That is why hierarchical systems, in the observation of their measures, depend on mechanisms such as various forms of collection, calculation and interpretation of data, formation of various models, among others. This aspect of observation is undoubtedly a very important one. However, over-reliance on mechanisms of observation of the environment in the formation of strategic orientations could even be used as an indicator of separateness and structural closure of the system from its environment. In this way systems rely on 'filtered' descriptions of an environment's operations. Meanwhile, structurally open systems can react directly to these operations happening in the environment:

> Organizationally closed systems respond to coordinated action and do that by structurally coupling themselves with their environment. Organizationally open systems can only respond to information (description of action) feedback *because*

they are not structurally coupled with their environment, but are separate or even isolated from it.

(Zeleny, 2001: 203)

Karl Deutsch showed that the efficiency and cohesiveness of societies depend on 'capacities of transferring information with more or less small losses of information' (Deutsch, 1969: 21, in Messner, 2013: 136). Because of this, the state must search for possibilities of making direct contact with its environment and decreasing its reliance on systems of 'filtered' information feedback.

The transition from socialist to post-socialist systems can also be observed from the perspective of chaotic processes in the framework of nonlinear systems. Various versions of planned economy as one of the forms of social systems are no exception. In the frame of opening to international trade, these nonlinear systems received some external inputs to their structure, which were strengthened by the mechanisms of a positive feedback loop to the point of the collapse of the system. At the beginning of the transition, the final consequences of these processes could not have been accurately predicted, or, one could say that numerous expectations about quick development that would follow the implementation of parliamentary democracies and that market economy have not been realised in all cases.

Influence of the complexity of environment on discussions about steering

Awareness about the inability of hierarchy as a key mechanism of steering of development began to penetrate discussions about the steering of social development. As far back as the 1960s, when the Keynesian model of macroeconomic management was still successful, Amitai Etzioni determined that strictly rational action is not possible in complex modern societies, because some necessary conditions are not fulfilled. According to Etzioni, these conditions are, first, to be informed about all possible directions of action and their consequences; second, to determine the consequences of these alternatives for various combinations of resources and simultaneously take into account various values; third, to have a consensus about values, based on which measures and consequences should be interpreted;

fourth, to make an exhaustive analysis of all alternatives. In view of such demanding conditions, the conclusion is clear: 'Societal bearers of decision-making don't have basic abilities for rational decision-making' (Etzioni, 1968: 264–265).

At the beginning of the 1970s, Fritz Scharpf published a text titled 'Complexity as an obstacle to political steering' (Scharpf, 1972) in which he problematised approaches that see hierarchical management as a technocratic problem that can be solved via the improvement of processes and increase of resources.

> Although politics in its information and decision-making system does achieve the level of differentiation of its own internal structures that suits the level of differentiation in the environment, it has always been proven, up to now, that is it very difficult, maybe even not completely doable, to reproduce actual co-dependencies, which exist in the problem context in socio-cultural environment.
>
> (Scharpf, 1972: 169)

In his opinion, this is the consequence of (in the language of systems theory) the political-administrative system not being able to establish 'structural coupling' (Luhmann, 1995; Zeleny, 1997; Zeleny, 2001) with its environment, which is of a socio-cultural nature. Political-administrative structures are not capable of facing the problem of complex mechanisms of co-dependence that exist in environment. These structures differentiate themselves by specialising individual units for particular problem domains. However, this specialisation is not upgraded with the establishment of co-ordination between these domains, which leads to inefficacy.

It is probably not difficult to find concrete examples of failures in the establishment of structural coupling. In making policies to promote economic development, policy-makers have to consider complex factors that influence the competitiveness of national economy; study on factors of competitive advantages of nations (Porter, 1990), which deals with the issue of differentiated influences of individual factors, or models of systemic competitiveness (Esser et al., 1996), which look for factors of developmental success on four different levels and in linkages between those four levels, bear witness to that fact. However, there are numerous obstacles to the successful linking between various ministries (of economy, of education, of science, etc.) or between administrative institutions on different levels (local, regional, national, supra-national).

Renate Mayntz identified reasons for the failure of such an approach:

> "Policy failure can be the consequence of cognitive mistakes in planning. Cognitive failure could involve data, theory, or both. Information about the details of a perceived problem could be insufficient, and policy decisions might be based on a wrong theory of the causal factors and causal connections at work in the policy field. Another cause of failure to reach a given policy goal can be the choice of an inadequate instrument, or the lack of appropriate resources, be they financial or legal. There are for instance, constitutional barriers to the choice of given political interventions, and budget constraints can stand in the way of introducing financial incentives, or engaging in costly programs of public provision. It was also recognized that the way policy-making is organized affects the substantive content of a policy."
>
> (Mayntz, 2016: 260).

She further cautioned that 'the best policy design can result in failure if its implementation is deficient' (Mayntz, 2016: 261), specifying that 'implementation does not simply mean the enactment of rules: deficits in the capacity of public administration, individual and organizational interests, and diverging normative convictions of the agents of implementation easily lead to divergence between policy goals and policy outcome' (ibid.).

Steering in Luhmann's systems theory

Niklas Luhmann is aware of the problem of growing complexity of social systems and he takes it into account when theorizing about mechanisms of social (self)steering:

> [...] "planning can only establish the premises of future behaviour, not the behaviour itself, which at the time of planning has not yet occurred....Besides, as system planning, planning must orient itself in some way to the system's complexity. It must make a model of the system, by which it can direct itself, thus introducing a simplified version of system's complexity into the system. This second complexity, this simplified second version of the system's complexity, emerges through planning".
>
> (Luhmann, 1995: 470).

Planning that is an attempt to confront a social system with the complexity of environment produces new, even higher levels of complexity. This results in a *hyper-complex* system, meaning system oriented towards its own complexity and by that 'it also creates new kinds of possibilities for unforeseen reactions' (Luhmann, 1995: 471). Because of this, planning cannot be an adequate mechanism for confronting the system with the complexity of environment. One possible solution to the growing complexity is unplanned differentiation of the system. Even forms of differentiation themselves depend on social evolution: '[...] the only forms of differentiation able to survive are those that can mobilize processes of deviation-amplification (positive feedback) to their own advantage [...]' (Luhmann, 1995: 190)

Differentiation and economy in modern societies

Differentiation of social systems is a solution with which society evolutionarily adapts itself to the growing complexity of environment (Luhmann, 1995: 189–191). Only those forms of differentiation that enable successful adaptation to growing complexity thus managed to preserve themselves in modern societies. Three different types of differentiation exist simultaneously in modern societies: segmentary, stratification, and functional differentiation (Luhmann, 1995). When describing various types of differentiation, Luhmann did not deal explicitly with the analysis of economic processes; however, all three types of differentiation play important roles in forming organisational forms and strategies for confronting the economy with the problem of complexity of the environment.

Segmentary differentiation

The first type of differentiation, described by Luhmann, is segmentary differentiation. It is 'differentiation into similar units (segmentation)' (Luhmann, 1995: 190), which means that when a particular system can no longer manage the complexity it experiences, it differentiates itself into numerous, mutually independent smaller units (which are similar to one another in hierarchical and functional sense) that can manage the complexity of environment more easily. Of course, significant differences in other aspects can exist between these units. Despite this type of differentiation preceding the other two types in the evolutionary sense, it is a type that remains rather important for analysis of steering of economic development.

Among the key developmental problems confronting the majority of developed societies are regional differences. The centralised state cannot confront this problem, which is in essence the problem of the complexity of environment, and thus the differentiation into smaller units that can more easily manage this complexity makes sense. This type of differentiation is even considered in the frame of European structural policies and the principle of subsidiarity. A typical example of such differentiation is regions, which represent the principle of division in the frame of structural policies of the European Union. Here it should be particularly emphasised that because of the principle of subsidiarity, which also applies to these developmental policies, segmentary differentiation has precedence over the stratification differentiation, which in the evolutionary sense emerges later, as a consequence of the growing complexity of the environment. Subsidiarity was implemented as a mechanism that was supposed to offer protection from excessive transfers of competences on the level of the European Union. This principle dictates that, if possible, decisions should be reached on lower levels: on national, regional, or even local levels. Decision-making is thus transferred to that level of subsidiary units that remain capable of successfully confronting the complexity and now also play an increasingly important role in innovation policy (Wanzenböck and Franken, 2020) contributing also towards the goals of sustainable development (Skivko, 2021).

Segmentary differentiation that evolved in primary human societies caused problems with the coordination of units, differentiated in such a way (Makarovič, 2001: 31). Today, this is less prevalent, as various forms of differentiation exist at the same time; moreover, segmentary differentiation is not a key type of differentiation in modern societies.

Stratification differentiation

Evolutionarily, stratification differentiation emerged later and, as such, it presupposes particular forms of coordination between differentiated units (Ibid: 32): specifically, hierarchical forms of coordination that enabled the formation of the first larger systems (early civilisations). In the beginning, stratification coordination was tied to the need for coordination that arose because the complexity of environment was such that individual, small separated multi-functional units could no longer manage it. However, with growing complexity, even this form of coordination became inadequate as it did not enable the adaptation of the system to the complexity of environment. With that, individual systems could no longer optimally perform their functions.

In the steering of economic development, stratification differentiation lost its former importance, as the hierarchical superiority of some subsystems (for example, political system) to the economic system leads to a situation in which the economic system can no longer adapt to its environment in line with its needs and criteria but must comply to external criteria. With that, optimal functioning becomes very questionable. For a hierarchically superior unit to be capable of performing its role in a complex environment, its complexity would have to reach the level of the complexity of environment; this is inherently impossible, as environment is always more complex than the system (Heyligen, 1992).

Despite that, one cannot completely neglect stratification differentiation because it is still present in some forms, and it even plays an important role in the frame of development of theories of organisations. An enterprise presents alternative coordination mechanism to the market, in the frame of which transaction costs, originating from social relations, are lowered (Williamson, 1975). While resources on the market allocate themselves with the help of price mechanisms, the mechanism of hierarchy is used in enterprises (Williamson, 1991); hierarchy plays an important part in research on big corporations (M-form) (Chandler, 1977). Hierarchical coordination can also be present in relations between enterprises, in the frame of monopsonistic clusters. In research on clusters, some authors emphasise the issue of power (Whittam and Danson, 2001) or at least highlight the need to take into account the unequal power relations that underpin interfirm relations (Cumbers et al., 2003). Despite that, stratification differentiation is less important in the formation of strategies of economic development because of the above-mentioned limitations originating in the complexity of environment.

Here, the difference between hierarchical superiority and centrality should be emphasised. Inequality between the units regarding resources does not equal stratification differentiation. Stratification differentiation also includes an ability to control and to steer (Makarovič, 2001: 33). However, such inequality regarding resources can be significant from the aspect of developmental steering. The unit that has greater resources can assume *central role* in strategic process. This role is not fulfilled with mechanisms of hierarchical intervention but by enabling, promoting, and coordinating between actors. This is especially important in cases where other actors are weak and do not have sufficient resources at their disposal. Examples of this are numerous developmental initiatives in underdeveloped or crisis areas, where international organisations perform their role in such a way (Rončević, 2002). In more developed societies, where the state has developed competencies and has sufficient resources at its disposal, the state itself can perform the role of central actor (*primus inter pares*).

Functional differentiation

In the first two forms of differentiation, a whole multifunctional system differentiates itself into smaller systems, which still perform numerous functions. In segmentary differentiation, each such individual system performs all functions that were previously performed by the whole. In stratification differentiation, new partial systems are, likewise, multifunctional, but there is differentiation in the steering and executive parts (Makarovič, 2001: 37). In the case of functional differentiation, new systems are formed on the basis of specialization in performing certain functions; every system performs a certain function and, at the same time, all systems are complementary to each other; together they perform all functions that would otherwise have to be performed by the whole.

Functional differentiation can be found on different levels. In modern societies, it is seen in the formation of economic, political, scientific, legal and similar systems on the macro level. On the mezzo level, functional differentiation is, for example, manifested through business clusters, in which individual organisations specialise in performing particular parts of the production process or certain accompanying services (research, employment agencies, business consultations and interventions, etc.). On the micro level, the existence of numerous specialized functions on the level of enterprises: production, finances, human resources management, marketing, and similar can be observed.

Functional differentiation is a characteristic of modern societies and can be an indicator of the level of modernity of individual society. In this sense, post-socialist societies can be described in terms of only partial or deformed modernity, due to the penetration of political system into other systems. With the help of this concept, we can also explain the formation of autonomous economic systems. Previously, these functions were performed by various multifunctional units, such as families or various forms of feudal units. Preconditions for the greater efficiency of individual partial systems emerged in the process of differentiation. The mechanism of functional differentiation itself is oriented toward greater efficacy, because it is not tied to external criteria in the process itself: 'with the transition to functional differentiation, the schematic of differentiation is chosen autonomously; it is directed only by the functional problems of the societal system itself, without any correspondences with the environment' (Luhmann, 1995: 193).

The three mentioned forms of social differentiation are complementary to each other. Segmentary differentiation in regions bears witness to that. Regions are, by definition, multifunctional units. However, these units also must face a highly complex environment. Consequently, they must differentiate themselves internally, which leads to hierarchical and functional differentiation. All three forms of differentiation can be found within the frames of larger enterprises as well (segmentary differentiation in the form of various branch offices, stratification differentiation in the form of superiority of some departments to others, functional differentiation in the form of specialisation of departments in performing various business functions). If some authors claim that functional differentiation is the criterion for modernity of specific societies: it could also be claimed that another criterion for modernity is the harmonisation of various forms of systemic differentiation. Here, Luhmann neglects the significance of other forms of differentiation in the steering of modern societies.

Functional differentiation leads to the autonomy of individual partial systems in the performance of its function. If this system loses its autonomy in the performance of its function because of the intervention of some other system (usually political), this can be termed regressive dedifferentiation. Therefore, social modernization has an interesting influence on abilities to steer these processes. On the one hand, differentiation implicates better capacities for confrontation with problems emanating from the complexity of environment. On the other hand, this is exactly the factor that can prevent successful steering if it comes to troubles with providing sufficient level of social integration in the form, where actors from various subsystems overemphasise the promotion of particularistic interests without regard to the needs of the system as a whole (Messner, 2013: 44). Processes of functional differentiation can thus lead either to 'active society' (Etzioni, 1968) or to its opposite: 'blocked society' (Crozier, 1970).

Role of politics in steering

Between the most often discussed examples, when self-reference of partial systems leads to troubles, are ecologic problems, produced by modern societies, especially in the context of economic systems. Luhmann concludes: 'Modern society's principle of differentiation makes the question of rationality more urgent – and at the same time insoluble. Any retreat to a traditional semantics of rationality would fail in the face of this situation' (Luhmann, 1995: 477). Nevertheless, he is of opinion that: 'Our outline of the problem of rationality does not assert that society must solve problems of this kind in order to survive. Evolution is all that is needed for survival' (Luhmann, 1995: 477). Luhmann's conclusion thus comes as no surprise: 'All planning is notoriously inadequate. It does not achieve its goals, or at least not to the extent that it would like, and it triggers side-effects it did not forsee' (Luhmann, 1995, p. 496).

> Based on the analysis of Luhmann's text, Makarovič concluded that Luhmann sees the following limitations of planning that originate from complexity (Makarovič, 2001: 124):
> • Limitations of possible knowledge and perceptions of planning,
> • Limitations of possibilities to implement planned measures, and
> • Growing complexity which originates from the process of planning itself.

According to Luhmann, the possibility of rational planning in modern societies is thus severely limited because of functional differentiation. Because of their own self-reference and operative closure, partial systems have difficulties in understanding the special needs of other systems that operate in accordance with different codes. Furthermore, a partial system is rather insusceptible to perceptions of systemic rationality (i.e., the needs of whole systems). The question arises of whether the system is even capable of reacting to measures that are supposed to intervene into it. If this measure does not take into account the specific code of an individual partial system, the system overlooks it. One example from the economy and research spheres: the stimulation of science as such does not lead to greater competitiveness of economy, if those measures are not oriented toward the stimulation of applicative research whose results can be understood by the economy (or concrete enterprises). Of course, the economy can also understand basic research, if it has such capacities; in this case, such investments are, of course, justifiable and lead to results. At this point, it must be underscored that planning itself leads to growing complexity of the system.

Luhmann's analysis of possibilities for steering in modern societies is very important, as it correctly points to numerous limitations and troubles that originate from the processes of functional differentiation; here Luhmann comes to conclusions similar to those of numerous other authors before him (Etzioni, 1968; Mayntz and Bohne, 1978; Scharpf, 1972). At the same time, his conclusions that social steering is not possible, are highly controversial (Makarovič, 2001: 124). If Luhmann's conclusions are a point of departure, then it could be maintained that in the context of modern societies, conventional hierarchical steering no longer possible; however, this tells us nothing about other forms of planned steering that exist in modern societies.

According to Luhmann, politics is no exception in regard to the processes of functional differentiation. It means that politics has been transformed from the hierarchical centre of society to a specialised partial system, which is not superior to others and does not have resources for steering other systems at its disposal; instead, it mainly can steer itself. Politics has become only one of a plurality social systems.

Luhmann does not pay sufficient attention to coordination that occurs (for which empirical evidence bears witness) between partial systems.

Refined mechanism of (self) steering: Helmut Willke

Helmut Willke, Luhmann's disciple, colleague, interpreter and, in many aspects, also his critic, revised chiefly those aspect of sociological systems theory that deal with the issues of steering of social development and with the role of the state or political system in steering. In his analysis, he rejected approaches that emphasis the significance of political systems and mechanisms of hierarchical intervention, as well as the adequacy of exclusive reliance on market mechanisms and spontaneous evolution – Luhmann's version of systems theory belongs among these.

> In developed societies creation of order ... is not solely the problem of the state anymore. Social order is only possible on the basis of specific mutual action of autonomous actors... Social order, based on hierarchy and planning is as obsolete as liberalistic formula of order, based on evolution, became dangerous.
>
> (Willke, 1992: 143)

In his discussions, Willke balances between apology for and revision of Luhmann's approach. At this point, we cannot deal in-depth with all aspects of his approach. We will not deal with those aspects that he resumed after Luhmann, but will limit ourselves primarily to those for which he revised Luhmann's approach, and especially on some of the most important innovations, particularly in description of three mechanisms of steering of social development that enable us to exceed autopoiesis, self-reference, and operative closure, which act as the greatest obstacle to social steering and lead into the blind alley of evolutionary development: reflexion, contextual intervention, and systemic discourse. Contrary to Luhmann, Willke does see the possibility of the reformation of the world (positivisation) and he even regards it as one of the three key indicators of modernity, alongside with functional differentiation and self-reference. That is why he is interested in 'sociological and social-theoretical relevance of the state and law as fundamental areas of social reality' (Willke, 1993: 34). It is not unimportant that possibility of steering the economy or partial systems in the frame of economy often finds itself in the centre of his analysis.

Reflexion

Functional differentiation and operative closure of partial systems create a need for integration and coordination. Of course, a need by itself does not make the establishment of such mechanism certain: needs must not be confused with causes (Makarovič, 2001: 40). The utilitarian inference, to which Luhamnn contributed, that partial systems are urged toward cooperation by need and interest for coordination is negated by empirical reality itself. Despite obvious proofs about numerous advantages of establishing horizontal and vertical links between enterprises (more on that in next chapter) or about the mutual usefulness of linking for enterprises as well as for research institutes, great differences in establishing cooperation between enterprises or between enterprises and research institutes exist (data in the annual *World Competitiveness Yearbook*, see also Adam et al., 2005a). The existence of ineffective institutional arrangements was successfully explained already in the 1990s in the frame of neo-institutional analysis in economy: as a consequence of transaction costs, connected to this (see North, 1990). The topic is still being discussed nowadays with the focus on the roles of new technologies (Frolov, 2020).

In analysing the dynamics of differentiation and integration. Willke concluded that while developed societies do react to the need for integration of functionally differentiated partial systems, this reaction is insufficient. The reason for this he sees in the problem that 'actors or subsystems have no need for coordination with other actors, unless if they put themselves into unusual position: if they see what they don't see and notice what they don't notice – namely the effects of their operations in their environment' (Willke, 1993: 111). This ability to conditionally exceed self-reference he describes as reflexion: 'observation of effects of one's own identity in the environment (including especially relevant reverse impacts of this effects on the system itself) in comparison with effects created by other systems in their environment' (ibid.: 113).

What does this mean for the steering of economic development? An important conclusion is that Wilke didn't relinquish the concept of self-reference. It means that in observing the environment, an enterprise or economic system as a whole can only interpret impulses in accordance with its specific code of action (e.g., market share, extent of production, profit). In this sense, Willke stays rather firmly in the frame of discourse that firmly separates the economic sphere and rationality, tied to it, from other spheres. However, such separation is not appropriate.

It is interesting that in cases of various negotiating mechanisms Willke notes that abilities for reflexion developed in various partial systems, but he explains them with the help of the principle of autopoiesis. Despite not excluding the actors from the analysis (unlike Luhmann), he completely neglects the obvious fact that actors trespass from one life-world to another. In modern societies, the economy is the system that is embedded into environment (Granovetter, 1985) and in which the influence of culture is particularly important. Evidence of this can be found on various levels. On the micro level, an enterprise represents one of the most dynamic areas of sociability, with individuals entering and exiting it more or less every day (workday). It would be illusory to expect that individuals would leave all their values and believes originating from their culture at the front doors of the enterprise. On the mezzo level, there is comprehensive evidence of intertwining between enterprises, research organisations, public administration, labour unions, and other entities, being the thickest in the most developed societies, where functional differentiation is highly developed. In socialist societies that dealt with important aspects of stratification differentiation, which eliminates the problem of social coordination by itself (social coordination is executed by hierarchically superior system) (Makarovič, 2001: 40), the thickness of such linkages is much lesser. Etzioni also states that modern societies are in fact more responsive to broader set of individual units than traditional societies were (Etzioni, 1968: 504).

Contextual intervention

Regardless of problems of closure, it is an empirical fact that even in highly complex societies particular systems successfully intervene into other systems. Here one first thinks of cases in which the political system interferes with other systems by mechanisms of hierarchical intervention. However, if we consider the principle of the decentralisation of society, then we also have to consider the possibility that there are cases in which actors of intervention are from other systems. In the context of this study, I am, of course, interested in capacities of the economy for intervention into other systems. Without doubt, the economy does make use of that. As an example, there is communication between enterprises and research institutions. In accordance with the principles of operative closure, they operate in compliance with principles of scientific research in the sense that no other system can determine scientific truth without danger of causing regressive dedifferentiation. Nevertheless, enterprises do influence the operation of scientific systems in a certain way; by financing particular studies they (in line with the economic logic of enterprises) stimulate researchers to work on certain scientifically relevant problems that would otherwise perhaps remain unaddressed. One could find a range of other examples, for example the policy of promoting business clusters (more on that in third chapter).

Certain possibilities of planned influence in other systems thus do exist. But one must ask what kind of intervention is needed in order for the system that it is supposed to influence it to recognise it as relevant and to not lead to systemic dedifferentiation or (through mechanisms of positive feedback loops) to the disintegration of a partial system.

To fulfil these two demanding criteria, political intervention (or intervention of any other system) has to be organised in such a way that it 'takes into account the operative closure and specific dynamics of individual systems. Interventions are thus possible only as a *conditioning of contextual conditions* that are included in the data basis of the systems, into which one intervenes, as noted differences' (Willke, 1993: 120, emphasis in original). Willke thus replaces the idea about linear causal steering, which is the least impossible because of the complex nature of social systems, but definitely rendered difficult and suboptimal, with the much softer idea about 'steering to self-steering'. As I will show later in the chapter about policies for strengthening social capital, contextual intervention is the only possible way to promote the development of intangible factors that cannot be strengthened with the help of conventional mechanisms for redistribution.

Systemic discourse

Reflexion and contextual intervention still have not entered the aspect of communication in relations between systems. This is the role of systemic discourse as the third mechanism of steering of modern societies, which enables the overcoming of operative closure and determination of guidelines of modern functionally differentiated societies: 'Systemic discourses mark the attempt to manage divergent rationalities and interests of organized and collective actors in negotiating systems' (Willke, 1993: 125). This is not about direct communications between partial systems; instead, it comes to creation of new 'negotiating' systems. The formation of these systems is also a part of the process of functional differentiation of modern societies and simultaneously a solution to the problems of social coordination that create them. Such negotiating systems can even develop their own autonomous logic.

In the frame of systemic discourse, actors (despite various interests) attempt to come to common solutions that satisfy specific needs of every partial system. While this is about particular forms of confrontation, this confrontation is limited by self-restricting behaviour of involved parties. Because this is about communication in the context of a decentralised society, no higher instance, leading, and directing this confrontation is present. In such communications '[...] actors have to lead themselves. They themselves have to define rules of their interaction and come to an agreement about validity of these rules' (Willke, 1993: 127). Willke is of the opinion that he solved the problems of communication between self-referential actors with the conceptualisation of three mechanisms of steering: 'Only linking of reflexion, contextual intervention and discourse enables the procedure in which the paradoxicalness of compatibility – not harmony! – can develop itself' (Willke, 1993: 125).

Here one must ask how Willke pictures the establishment of the mutual communication of functionally differentiated subsystems or actors. In his theoretical approach, one can find certain inconsequentialities or even clear inconsistencies originating from the fact that he does not explicitly relinquish certain aspects of Luhmann's 'orthodoxy'; here, one can mention especially the concepts of self-reference, autopoiesis, and operative closure (see Adam, 1996: 234–236). Willke sees communication as a 'transfer of understandable information' (Willke, 1993: 100) that occurs when a system understands offered information and accepts it. It can only understand it when information is adapted to its specific code.

It seems that Willke, despite important conceptual innovations, remains too moderate in his conclusions. In his opinion, the principal function of discourse is not the creation of consensus (discourses are headed toward dissensus) but the generation of information that can be understood by specialised partial systems; with that, systems also understand the influence of their own actions on environment and returning influence of the environment on the actions of partial system (Ibid: 128). However, with that, he does not solve the question of how this new partial system can generate information understandable to all other self-referential, autopoietic, and operatively closed systems, in the first place.

It must be emphasised that Willke understands the concept of consensus very narrowly: as a common truth or common criterion of correctness. With this, he implicitly presupposes the situation of a zero-sum game, in which the systems with divergent interests are not supposed to be able to come to formation of common interests. However, everyday empirical evidence confirms that that search for consensus as an agreement about common interests on the basis of divergent interests is actually possible (e.g., in successful examples of social dialogue). If one comprehends the self-reference of partial systems as absolute, as Luhmann does and which Willke does not renounce, then systemic discourse is impossible, as is the strategic steering of development. Empirical evidence, of course, indicates that absolute self-reference does not exist and that the level of closure of individual systems is an empirical question (Adam, 1996). Critics searched for the solution of this dilemma in the concept of *transference*, which Willke introduced into his theory with the concept of 'transferential operation'. The concept of transference describes systems that are simultaneously open and closed:

> These still preserve some internal autonomy, but with reference to them, one cannot talk about asymmetry between closure and openness or about primacy of closure (self-reference) [...]. Only systems defined in such a way are capable of surpassing their own identity in the sense of ability for reflexion on the basis of empathy [...]. Only this enables partial system to become aware of effects of its operations on environment... and to reconstruct self-description of other partially systems as an observer. This is point of departure for instructive interaction and systemic discourse, without which we cannot even imagine steering in the sense of functional coordination.

(Adam, 1996: 236)

An economic system that must also be able to interpret those impulses from the environment that are not entirely in accordance with its specific systemic code is also necessarily placed between transferential systems. The above-mentioned case of fundamental science that can also be interesting for economy bears witness to the ability of economy to develop mechanisms for the understanding or translation of other codes. One of the most typical cases is the peaceful usage of nuclear energy, which was based on theoretical physics. The economy is probably the transferential system *par excellence*, which must pay attention to numerous impulses from the environment and understand them.

It is difficult to avoid the impression that Willke, because of his opposition to some aspects of Luhmann's theory, did not develop his analysis to the level that he could have. Numerous conclusions of sociological systems theory are undoubtedly true. Two evolutionary principles (functional differentiation and operative closure) can represent the problem of modern society. The first leads to growing interdependence between actors, and the second leads to their increasing closure. However, this growing of dependence and independence is precisely the cause for growing density of communications. Analysis should be furthered by searching for answers to questions about the basis of these communications. Concretely, why can linkages that contribute to stimulation of economic development (neocorporatist negotiating systems, links between organisations in the frame of business clusters, etc.) establish themselves in certain environments? What is the common semantic frame on which the *transference* of social systems is based? The question of *common semantic frame* that enables transferential operations in the first place did not attract Willke's attention.

Network phenomena: Toward the upgrade of systemic analysis

Both discussed approaches in the frame of systems theory without doubt have important explanatory potentials in steering of modern societies. However, their approach – especially Luhmann's – sometimes does not have very good contact with reality. When reading their texts, an uncritical reader might think that modern societies are completely disintegrated and are on the brink of collapse. Nevertheless social systems in modern societies are surprisingly stable and able to establish robust in the context of an exceptional variety of inter-systemic communications and relations between individual and collective actors. This confirms that processes of functional differentiation do not lead to social disintegration but instead create conditions for the formation of more complex forms of social coordination within networks. That is why these approaches have to be used in such a way that one can start answering the questions they pose; these questions are also the most interesting and strongest part of this theory: 'Luhmann's questions are more interesting than his answersp (Messner, 2013: 104), specifically the question about foundations of communications between partial systems and preconditions for these communications – and with that also about preconditions of strategic steering of development. At the beginning of the 1990s, Fritz Scharpf stated that:

> In the light of present state of the theory it seems that need to explain the growing of everywhere noticeable chaos is lesser than the measure of intra- and inter-organizational, intra- and inter-sectional coordination and reciprocal certainty of expectations that *exists despite everything*. Beyond the market, the hierarchical state and discourses about control there are obviously increasingly efficacious mechanisms of coordination and steering in internally differentiated and internationally integrated modern societies than scholars empirically discovered and theoretically grasped up until now.
>
> (Scharpf, 1993: 57, emphasis in original)

The concept of network implies self-organisation and self-coordination that established themselves between autonomous actors. 'These network forms of organization and steering, based on them, can be interpreted as reaction to phenomena of increasing social, political and economic differentiation, specialization and interdependence' (Messner, 2013: 148). It could thus be said that networks (connection, communication, and cooperation that occur within these frames) solve essential problems of social modernisation. In this sense, research on networks represents an upgrade of sociological systems theory. This theory was unsuccessful because of limitations presented to it by aforementioned concepts, which (empirically unfoundedly) presupposed the absolute exclusion of the environment from the system. Social modernisation does not presuppose such exclusivity but represents the motor of formation of the network type of organising. Because of this, networks are the essential expression of social modernisation (Mayntz, 1993) and key to understanding of fundamental social structures (Messner, 2013: 178).

Messner (2013: 180) states that networks are innovations that can solve complex problems that cannot be successfully confronted by conventional forms of steering. Market forms of allocations can produce negative externalities and, more importantly, long-term strategic visions of intentional action cannot be reached by market mechanisms. At the beginning of this chapter, I discussed the limitations or even inabilities of hierarchical steering in the conditions of high complexity. In contrast, the functional logic of networks is characterised by the combination of elements of these two basic patterns and, as such, it represents higher level of action. This is characterized by: (1) the existence and action logic of autonomous, decentrally organised actors, which appear on the market (at least in ideal type) and (2) action strategy, which is oriented toward definition of mezzo- and long-term common goals and toward definition of resources needed for achieving of these goals.

The comprehension of the growing presence of these phenomena started in studies within the frame of approaches that analyse policy networks. These approaches are relatively new and have not yet constituted themselves in the form of a new school or structured approach, such as can be said for two fundamental orientations that can be distinguished by the distinction market versus the state. Currently, there is an agreement about what policy networks actually are. Is this a metaphor, a methodological approach, an analytical method, or even a real theory?

Despite that, a quick overview of bibliographical data easily reveals that the notion of the network became very present not merely in research on the steering of development and not even in social science. This concept is (similarly to the concept of system) useful for application in various sciences. A common denominator of these various uses is dealing with complex problems. The notion of the network became, so to speak, 'a new paradigm of architectural complexity' several decades ago (Kenis and Schneider, 1991: 25).

> [...] network perspective implies new perception of causal relations in social pro-
> cesses [...]. The core of this perspective is decentralized concept of social organi-
> zation and steering [...]. Mechanisms of control are dispersed and information is
> distributed across a multitude of action units. Coordination of these units is not
> a result of "central steering" or certain type of in advance determined harmony
> any more, instead it establishes itself in intentional interactions of individual ac-
> tors that are qualified for parallel action with the exchange of information and
> other relevant resources.
>
> (Kenis and Schneider, 1991: 26)

Here we will not discuss the expansive problems of analysis of forms of policy networks in more detail (for that see Rhodes, 2007; Blanco et al., 2011, etc.). Possibilities for the use of this conceptual frame are numerous and have been extensively explored in recent decades. Granovetter researched the role of weak and strong networks in career paths (Granovetter, 1973) and role of social networks in the development of Silicon Valley (Castilla et al., 2000). Walker and co-authors researched the establishment of industrial networks (Walker et al., 1997). Nieto and Santamaria analysed the role of different types of collaborative networks in achieving product innovations and their degree of novelty (Nieto and Santamaria, 2007). Similarly, Zeng and colleagues were interested in the relationships between different cooperation networks and the innovation performance of small- and medium-sized enterprises (Zeng et al., 2010). Ranchod and Vas (2019) focused on the need for better linkages between evidence and policymaking, discussing the utility of a policy community network between academic researchers and policymakers. This conceptual frame was also often used in research on transitional processes in post-socialist Europe (Benton et al., 2015; Angelusz and Tardos, 2001; Grabher and Stark, 1997).

We are more interested in the question of preconditions for the possibilities of efficacious network linkages. A minimal common semantic frame (i.e., a system that wishes to intervene into other system has to understand and consider the conditions that determine its operating) and an ability for reflexion and learning must exist.

Society of networks and developmental dynamics

'Network phenomena' can thus be explained as a consequence of modernization trends, which, more than in the case of segmentary and stratification differentiation, put modern societies before the question of social integration. These processes also led to the lessening of the probability of successful hierarchical coordination and successfulness of spontaneous evolution. Networks can offer part of the solution to the problems of social coordination that originate from developmental dynamics of modern societies. Transformational processes that accompany social modernisation led to the strategic process of formation of network forms. I summarize Messner's description of these trends (2013: 150–153):

1. *Trend in the direction of organising society.* The numbers of collective actors and their influence on the steering of social development

and acceleration of developmental dynamics are growing. Advantages derived from linking also include the pooling of limited resources and combining various competences and forming new, emergent ones that exceed the sum of resources of individual actors.

2. *Increasing sectorisation of economy and society.* This is about a process that we have termed 'functional differentiation'. Complementary process of specialisation occurs with this process. This leads to establishment of conditions for increasing importance of individual partial systems or individual actors in society.

3. One consequence of the inclusion of these actors in the process of decision-making is the *supersaturation of the policy process.*

4. Differentiation of partial systems leads to *the growth of policy.* It means that because of the risks emanating from the decline of systemic rationality on account of target rationality, am increasing volume of state interventions occurs (there are more and more domains and possible situations that have to be regulated). At the beginning, there were no sufficient attempts of innovative forms of steering, and this led to (over)load of the state.

5. In the long run, this process led to the *decentralisation and fragmentation of the state,* meaning that various forms of intervention and steering started to emerge in the framework of the state. Shifting the responsibility to lower levels (regional, local) also occurred.

6. With decentralisation, came various forms of cooperation between the state and other actors. *The border between policymakers and recipients of policies became blurred.*

7. In some domains, developments led to the state completely losing its abilities for the autonomous making of policies. Input from other actors cannot be neglected without consequences for the quality of formed measures. It resulted in *the loss of the autonomy of the state inwards.* This is not just a conventional loss of the autonomy because of the processes of globalisation and regionalisation but also about a loss of the autonomy in the relation to other partial systems.

8. From this arose the need for *the cooperative or negotiating state* that has to learn to impart responsibility to lower levels and other actors and, of course, to support the capacities of these actors for successful cooperation in policy processes.

9. Conditions for *active society* (Etzioni, 1968), in which strategic processes occur in the interaction between relevant actors and partial systems, are established based on previous trends. This is simultaneously the only successful solution to growing mutual dependency. These interactions establish relations of inter-systemic coordination that differ from market or hierarchical relations.

10. Globalisation, the regionalisation of the economy, and the integration of national states into supra-national organisations contribute to *the loss of the autonomy of the state outwards*.

Different explanations of formation of new forms of social coordination also exist. The most famous of them is the approach of technological determinism, which Manuel Castells explained at the beginning of his most famous work 'The Rise of the Network Society': 'A technological revolution, centred around information technologies, began to reshape, at accelerated pace, the material basis of society. Economies throughout the world have become globally interdependent, introducing a new form of relationship between economy, state and society' (Castells, 1997: 1). In this sense, Castells also explained the downfall of socialistic systems as a consequence of their inability to adapt to demands that of the information technology revolution put before them (Castells, 1998). In this, he made a thesis statement similar to that of Berend, who states in his texts that East European societies developmentally lag behind because they are not capable of adapting to the demands that are put before them by continually emerging new industrial revolutions (Berend and Ranki, 1982; Berend, 2001). Despite different point of departure, he came to similar conclusions about the role of the state and forms of policy processes.

Steering role of the state in network society: Primus inter pares

At the beginning of the 1990s, David Held stated that society is dealing with a hybrid system, in which the system of sovereign national states persists despite different trends as systems of plural structures are also simultaneously developing (Held, 1991). The nation-state represents only one of the existing centres of power in a broader network, where it often confronts other centres that limit its autonomy (Castells, 1998: 304). This is even more so the case with the European Union, whose regulatory powers are being constrained and defined by the Member States. However, this does not mean that the decline of the nation-state is coming, but it does indicate a change in execution of the role which state can play in strategic processes: '...while global capitalism flourishes and national ideologies throughout the world explode, it seems that national state, created in modern era, loses its power, but, and this is essential, *not also its influence*' (Castells, 1998: 243; emphases in the original quote).

As I have already stressed, the state not only loses its autonomy outwards but also inwards. Castells states that subordinate social groups gain access to policy processes, especially on lower levels. 'Thus, a complex geometry emerges in the relationship between the state, social classes, social groups, and identities present in civil society' (Castells, 1997; 271). In this way, lower levels, the so-called 'local state', become important strategic instances. In this way, local and regional governments become manifestations of decentralised political power, points of contact between the state and other social subsystems. Networks, within which policies are made, become much more complicated. An example of this is presented by the policies of European Union with the principle of subsidiarity, which complicates the analysis of networks with the introduction of analysis of multilevel steering (Stephenson, 2013; Eberlein and Kerwer, 2004).

Hirst and colleagues (2009) also criticise those simplifying visions that see reasons for the irrelevance of the nation-state in economic globalisation and the rise of the power of multi-corporations. As literature about the 'localization' of competitive advantages indicates, the role of nation-states really is changing, internally (relations between central, regional, and local levels) as well as towards other actors. Instead of traditional macroeconomic measures that are necessary but insufficient conditions for economic competitiveness, other factors, which can only develop in cooperation of various actors, come forward.

> The emerging forms of governance of international markets and other economic processes involve the major national governments but in a new role: states will come to function less as all-purpose providers of governance and more as the authors and legitimators of an international 'quasi-polity'; the central functions of the nation-state will become those of providing legitimacy for and ensuring the

accountability of supranational and subnational governance mechanisms which exercise various forms of 'private' authority.

(Hirst et al., 2009: 220–221)

Linda Weiss noted that reaction of the state to these pressures of functional differentiation was not uniform. Regarding political-institutional differences, two answers formed. In both cases, it is about the upgrade of coalitions: 'upwards', in the direction of the construction of interstate coalitions on regional and broader levels, and 'downwards', in the direction of formation of coalitions with internal actors, for example in the form of connections with the economy. She termed states that avail themselves of building of these coalitions 'catalytic states'. This means that in reaching goals, these states do not lean predominantly on their own resources (this is what 'integral states' do); instead, they attempt to reach them as a central or dominant partner in the frame of coalitions of states, transnational institutions, or private actors, in which they attempt to be indispensable link of particular strategic coalitions and, at the same time attempt to stay relatively independent in relation to other actors (Weiss, 1998).

The nation-state in a network society finds itself under pressure from very different actors, spanning from capital and production networks to supranational structures and organised crime (Castells, 1997: 304). However, this does not mean that those actors successfully exercise their influence or strengthen their autonomy. Shrinking the autonomy of the state does not presuppose automatic strengthening of the autonomy of other actors (Messner, 2013: 151–152). The example of post-socialist societies clearly bears witness to this: actors have insufficient resources and consequently cannot affect the potentials derived from systemic transformation. Nielsen and co-authors thus stated that 'post-socialist state [...] has to increase powers to reduce powers' (Nielsen et al., 1995: 11). The strategic capacity of individual actors and constellations of relationships between them are those two factors that determine their role in social steering. Questions about the actual role of individual actors or partial systems can be answered by empirical analysis. About the actual role of the state in steering of social development, we can make inferences only on the basis of an analysis of strategic competencies of actors.

Suppositions for networks

Numerous analyses about market failure in coordination exist in the literature about market and state. In this study, I indicate some suppositions and circumstances of failure of hierarchical forms of steering. Of course, networks must not be regarded as a 'panacea', as a universal formula that can solve problems of integration and steering in modern societies. In the literature, one can find quite a few cases that indicate that the existence of networks does not suffice for successful steering by itself or that networks can also have negative impacts. Banfield's case study of small village in the south of Italy the 1950s, which he named 'Montegrano', can be considered a classical study. In this case study, he researched the overly strong connections of family networks, which were not upgraded with extensive networks on other levels ('amoral familism') and hindered cooperation and socio-economic development (Banfield, 1959). Gambetta's study (1989) about mafia networks and studies that focus on researching negative aspects of social capital (Pillai et al., 2015, Labianca and Brass, 2006; Portes, 1998) can also be placed among such studies. In contrast, the possibility of the direct failure of networks as a mechanism of social steering is also important. The coordination of relationships in networks is most sophisticated; consequently, it puts the most difficult demands before the members of network. This is demonstrated by an example of cooperation in an enterprise. Of three forms of internationalisation (passive, autonomous, and cooperative) the third is the most difficult and simultaneously the least likely one, although it would be (in principle) the most wished-for one because of the speed of internationalisation. This poses set of questions to members of network: question of trust between partners, question of control, fear of partners' power (abuse of dominant position), and similar. Because of this, the possibility of network failure should also be addressed here.

Within networks, numerous causes can lead to failure (Messner, 2013). The first is the problem of the number of actors in network. If there are too many, negotiating processes for reaching of consensus become impossible: with the increased number of actors, the possibility for reaching consensus, satisfactory for all, decreases. Second, a question occurs in the time dimension: can an institutional environment guarantee that formed strategies do not follow short-term impulses but are instead oriented toward long-term goals? Third, there is a problem of institutional consolidation of networks. After the beginning phase, network consolidations and exits from the network can have significant costs for the one exiting from it. This puts actors under the pressure to stay in the network even after the membership is no longer optimal for them and does not fulfil their needs. Because of this, members of network can be forced to make compromises that paralyse common action. Fourth, problems of coordination arise also because compromising to improve common benefits is rendered severely difficult, if consensus does not bring individual benefits that surpass the status quo for every individual member of network. Fifth, particular 'motivational' factors for the efficacy of networks exist. Mutual trust and cooperative orientation are of key importance here, but they are put to the test when question about division of costs and benefits arises. Sixth, there is the question of power. In the network, resources are usually unevenly distributed. Particular actors have strategic resources that are more important than resources of other actors. Networks are not *a priori* free and democratic, and asymmetry of power can lead to erosion of cooperative orientation. Seventh, both conflict and cooperation appear in the network simultaneously. Balance between the two is optimal. Excessive 'harmony' can paralyse innovation potentials, while excessive conflict leads to paralysation of decision-making and disintegration.

All the above-mentioned problems can lead to blocked decision-making or to structurally conservative action orientation. However, empirical evidence bears witness to the fact that in some environments network failure occurs more frequently than in others. Analysis of networks cannot satisfactorily explain why this is so. In this sense, such analysis did not markedly succeed in surpassing the deficiencies of sociological systems theory. In searching for an answer to these questions, authors of approaches that focus on socio-cultural presuppositions of behaviour, especially on the role of social capital and culture, were much more successful.

However, until quite recently, the sociological literature has generally sought only to explain the conditions under which network forms of organisation are functional while largely ignoring what happens when those conditions are not present. Schrank and Whitford (2011) attempted to fill this gap by developing a theory of 'network failure', thereby contributing to the development of sociology's toolkit for theorising about networks that are 'neither market nor hierarchy'. They provided a candidate framework that establishes the social conditions of network governance (i.e., institutional safeguards against incompetence and opportunism) and distinguishes between two types of *absolute* network failures that occur in extreme cases of their joint absence or underdevelopment: (1) the breakup of already existing relationships, which they refer to as *network devolution*; and (2) the nonappearance of potentially profitable or productive networks, which they refer to as *network stillbirth*. They then identified two varieties of *relative* network failure that occur when one, but not both, of the aforementioned safeguards is absent or relatively underdeveloped: (1) networks can 'permanently fail' due to a lack of competencies, in which case they label the network *involuted*; (2) or they can 'permanently fail' due to opportunism, in which case they label the network *contested*. Finally, they showed that while each of these forms of network failure is in a sense distinct, they can nonetheless be usefully and systematically related to each other and to existing theories of network governance. Their theory thus views network failures not as the simple absence of network governance but rather as a situation in which transactional conditions for network desirability obtain but network governance is impeded either by ignorance or opportunism, or by a combination of the two and depicts network failures as continuous rather than discrete outcomes.

Innovation 2.0 for smart and inclusive growth: Towards intentional strategic action

In the 20th century, after Schumpeter elaborated his statement regarding the competition and delivering a model of innovation occurrence (Gangaliuc, 2019), the concept of innovation entered scientific and policy debates. Since then, innovation has become the central focus of authors such as Porter (1990) and Granovetter (1985) who conceptualised reliance of the phenomenon on the networks. This has been further elaborated, for example in the framework of SOFIA approach to innovations (Rončević et al., 2022), which allows us to develop nuanced analyses of the interplay of networks, institutions, and cognitive frames in processes of innovation (Modic and Rončević, 2018; Rončević and Modic, 2011). In the context of development (especially economic development), the concept gained attention of all stakeholders of the Quadruple Helix. The economic realities developed to the point where the innovation performances need to be shown on all levels of societies; for social scientists, the main question emerged on how to conceptually grasp the phenomenon and its manifestations.

However, economic realities can widely differ, especially if in the countries of so-called Danube region. These are the countries covered by the Danube Transnational Programme through its Interreg Danube instrument (Besednjak Valič, 2019; Cepoi, 2019; Besednjak Valič et al., 2021; Besednjak Valič et al., 2020). The programme addresses the set of highly developed parts of Germany (Baden Wurttemberg and Bavaria) as well as the least-developed parts of EU instrument ENI (Moldova, parts of Ukraine). To be able to enhance development and foster innovation throughout such regions, the EU is encouraging the processes of digital transformation; however, the need for more strategies and locally based approaches is often seen. To better understand the processes the EU, knowledge of the organisation, functioning, and changing of social systems is vital.

To be able to reach the ambitious developmental goals of the EU, past events need to be taken into account, specifically the initial grand strategy document. Starting with the Lisbon Strategy, later with Europe 2020, the

EU is aiming to achieve smart, sustainable, and inclusive growth (Rončević, 2020; Makarovič et al., 2014). Alongside the strategies, tools for their implementation have been developed substantially (e.g., Smart Specialisation Strategy). Currently, Agenda 2030 and its Sustainable Development Goals are the relevant EU macro-strategy. The authors dealing with analysis of effectiveness of these documents are numerous and address the issue from different angles (Saunila, 2017, 2019; Pandiloska Jurak, 2019; Rončević, 2019; Rončević, 2020). Two interesting aspects of discussion are noted from the perspective of high-tech companies (Pandiloska Jurak, 2020) outlining their role in the processes of implementation of Horizon 2020 strategic goals and contributions addressing the ecological and environmental challenges (Uršič, 2020; Fric, 2019) and proposed solutions through circular economy paradigm. However, when it comes to exploring innovation systems, interesting research by Hafner and Modic (2020) is worth mentioning, as it sheds a light of the state of the art of the technological innovation systems of Slovenia, Hungary, and Austria with emphasis on the relationships between the actors who are part of European automotive supply chains. As innovation environments are changing (ibid), the framework conditions for innovative enterprises also change and that includes the fields of entrepreneurship and academic entrepreneurship (Modic et al., 2022). As Erman (2020) concludes, it was the 2004–2016 period when specific conditions related to funding of innovation companies improved, although the question of human capital remain an issue. Apart from that, the role of social capital was emphasised with the same amount of importance (Pandiloska Jurak, 2021) along with organisational co-governance (Zdravje, 2021).

Systems theory is, on account of subscribing to the concept of autopoiesis of social systems, oriented mainly toward research on non-intentional and recursive action. However, innovative processes are *per definitionem* intentional actions. Moreover, Innovation 2.0 for smart and inclusive growth is even more so, on a more complex scale, since it is based on the Quadruple Helix Model in which government, businesses, academia and civil society collaborate to co-create the positive societal change (i.e. innovation) and drive structural changes far beyond the scope of what any one organization or person could do alone. This model thus renders obsolete the idea non-intentional and recursive action.

Despite that, some starting points for research on possibility of strategic steering of social development and course of strategic process do exist in the frame of systems theory. In addition to Willke's above-mentioned innovations, two concepts that were offered by Luhmann in the frame of his theoretical opus can also be mentioned. The first is the concept of *episode*, with which he denotes the sequence of structured communication, with which organisations temporarily stop routine structures of discourse, communication and hierarchy; in this way, they open the place for reflexive strategic practice (Luhmann, 1995: 268). In this sense, with this concept we can embrace all those aspects of dynamics of strategic processes in which we deal with rather consistent and permanent manners of confronting of a social system with environment (autopoiesis), which interrupted is in certain circumstances by rather radical strategic redirection (episodes). The second concept, which Luhmann explicitly ties to the concept of strategy, is the concept of *programme*. 'Programs can be designated as strategies if and insofar as one provides for them to change, on occasion, while they are being carried out' (Ibid.: 577). The specification of information is thus an opportunity for changing certain aspects of the programme, which can change in advance determined selection between options.

However, the mentioned concepts cannot be used for the analysis of developmental steering. First, using both concepts, especially the concept of episode, in the frame of Luhmann theoretical opus is rather 'episodic' and these two concepts do not occupy the most important position. Consequently, he did not develop theoretically important consequences in more detail. From the viewpoint of our discussion, it is also important that Luhmann attributes the capacity for production of episodes (and with this, intentional strategic changes) to psychic systems (Luhmann, 1995: 268) and, in accordance with his theoretical orientation, neglects the possibility of strategic action of partial systems.

The significance of these two concepts is (similarly to Willke's conceptual innovations) in highlighting important questions about the social presuppositions of processes of strategic steering. First, regarding Luhmann's supposition about the acentric nature of the society, one must question suppositions and the course of processes of constituting strategic programme on the level of society. In this context, who the 'holder' of this programme is also an important question As the concept of programme also embraces orientation towards goals or conditions of action, this is at the same time question about which actors take part in determining these goals (legitimacy of goals) and in their execution. Second, it highlights the discussion about the relation between intentional strategic action and structural obstacles that originate from the (social and cultural) environment. In strategic episodes it is important that, despite temporary stoppages of routine structures of discourse and self-reproduction of systems, these processes do not occur in a vacuum but are based on sedimentary preceding interactions (Golob and Makarovič, 2017). With the help of episodes, social structures that are non-congruent with the already existing ones can form; in this way, episodes contribute to subsequent sedimentation and structuration of this environment. In this chapter, we will deal with these questions.

Towards the concept of a strategy of societal development

Studies of strategic steering have a rich tradition in social sciences; some specifics with important consequences for studies of social development are apparent. First, the concept of strategy as a form of social action is relatively poorly defined (Whittington, 1993). Consequently, difficulties while studying strategic steering exist. Key problems are related to the delimitation of the research object, which leads to incomparable operationalisations, data, and conclusions. These problems are aggravated by the fact that in more recent, sociologically oriented approaches (i.e., strategy as practice approach) the object of research by definition surpasses the limits of a specific organisation or subsystem and includes the fields of culture and values. Additionally, due to the smaller relevance of hierarchical forms of steering, strategy-making process cannot be ascribed only to specific 'strategists'. Consequently, almost every activity taking place in the organisation, subsystem, or society can be studied as a part of strategic practice (Hendry and Seidl, 2002:3).

Second, most studies in this field focus on research of individual profit or non-profit organisations (companies, administrative institutions, NGOs, etc.). In this sense, most of this literature belongs to the narrow field of strategic management. More sociologically oriented approaches attempt to integrate micro and macro approaches. However, these attempts are guided primarily by the interest in the impact of the wider socio-cultural field on specific strategic practices occurring in specific organisations (Whittington, 2002). While studying the steering of social development, we need to have an interest in the mutual effect of both levels.

We should also emphasise some common traits. First, in the framework of both studies of organisational strategies and studies of strategic steering of social development, there is a need for a reduction of complexity. Strategy is *a tool for the reduction of complexity.* An economic system is not a trivial subsystem: it is a complex subsystem, and this quality influences the ability to steer developmental trajectories. Organisations are also complex systems, and this complexity has to be reduced: there is a need for a reduction of possible options to select. Strategy reduces complexity to the extent that it is possible to select between options that emerge in the system and in the environment. In this sense, we can understand strategy as 'the activity of selecting, and selectively combining, forms of complexity reduction' (Seidl, 2003: 3). Selection between different options can lead to either declarative or authentic *consensus about the goal* we are to achieve; selection renders other options (at least temporarily) irrelevant.

Second, strategy is a concept that enables us to deal with the theoretical and practical consequences of social changes. In this sense, we can understand strategy *as activity to steer changes.* Here, we come close to sociological theories of social practice, which deal with interrelationships between the macro-level (societal structures) and micro-level (actors). During strategic processes, there is more or less successful implementation of *control over changes*; in the context of this study, it is control over social changes.

When attempting to answer whether society is capable of establishing strategic steering processes, we have to answer the question of whether it is capable of establishing, first, a developmental consensus and second, control over developmental processes. Goal setting is a relatively simple process with companies and other types of organisations. These are determined by stakeholders, who are in many cases external factors (i.e., owners, members, founders etc.) These goals are also more or less clearly defined (i.e., as a profit market share, services output, etc.). Even in cases of family businesses, which can be quite distinctive from other types of enterprises, specific goal setting (i.e., employment and decent income for family members) can be observed. Control over the achievement of goals is relatively simple; the capability of implementing strategy is measured by proxy (i.e., the achievement of set goals). On the macro system or sub-system level, there is an inability to do so, as legitimate goals cannot be set by some 'supreme' instance in contemporary societies. Any such goals can be declaratively determined, but in such a case their implementation is questionable.

The ability to build consensus about developmental trajectories and the capability of societies to control its implementation are, according to Amitai Etzioni (1968), a key dimension of social steering. He analytically distinguishes four categories of societies, according to these two criteria:

1. *Passive societies* are societies with low ability to build developmental consensus and a low level of control over development. This group of countries consists mostly of poorly developed societies (e.g., Third World).
2. *Over-managed societies* are societies with a high level of control and a low level of developmental consensus. There are many such countries, especially among various authoritarian regimes. A high level of social control does not necessarily imply effectiveness. In many cases, there are omnipresent, but weak states, with a negative impact on economic development and entrepreneurial initiatives.
3. *Drifting societies* are societies with a high level of developmental consensus and a relatively low level of control. Western democratic societies are typical examples of this category.
4. *Active societies* are societies with a high level of developmental consensus and a high level of control over developmental trajectories.

This typology implies that active societies are those that have the capacity for strategic steering of social development. Active societies are Etzioni's normative ideal, as they enable the influence of all relevant social actors and not only those with the biggest social power; this is the only authentic consensus (Makarovič, 2001: 169). Including all relevant and interested actors is not only relevant to ensure social justice and equality but also to contribute to solving technocratic problems, which emerge while formulating and executing (control) developmental strategies (Golob et al., 2016). Societies that quickly combine the goal of successful economic development (growth) with social cohesiveness and cultural prosperity are societies that solve their dilemmas through organisational and political pluralism (Messner, 2013). There are some specific and very successful examples of undemocratic states in East Asia (steering development as developmental states), where authorities legitimised themselves through economic development. However, in addition to remark that it is difficult to talk about cultural prosperity and quality of life in view of obvious repression and violation of human rights, we can also observe that these undemocratic consensus-building processes contributed to development of negative externalities (e.g., development of militant trade union movements). Economic development led to either democratisation (South Korea, Taiwan) (Castells, 1998), or knowledge about negative impacts of paternalism, hindering inventiveness and creativity, which are in fact a necessary condition for most sophisticated production processes.

This implies that successful developmental strategies are formulated and implemented in constant interlinkage and dialogue (both formal and informal) of all relevant actors. Equal dialogue between partners is a necessary condition of a successful strategic process. Elinor Ostrom writes about 'coproduction', which describes the joint involvement of public and private actors in productive processes, where both sides make their contribution (Ostrom, 1997). When the contribution of both actors is complementary, cooperation can lead to significant synergetic effects. Peter Evans (1997) also emphasises the possibility of synergy stemming from the cooperation between state and society.[8] He emphasises two basic principles. The first is complementarity, as with Ostrom's approach. By 'complementarity', he describes mutually supportive relationships between private and public actors. This also presupposes a clear division of work, which is based on the qualities and competences of individual actors. The second is the concept of embeddedness, describing linkages between public and

---

8   Evans adopts a Hegelian notion of society, i.e. everything not in the state. This also includes, for example, civil society, rural communities, the business sector, etc.

private actors.[9] The application of this concept makes analysis of strategic processes more difficult, as numerous interactions presuppose establishment of formal and informal institutional and arrangements and networks, which can have both positive and negative consequences. However, at the same time, they increase the possibility of building authentic consensus and successful control over development. Therefore, the cooperation of competent strategic actors is essential for processes of strategic steering. Evans discusses the need for communication between a strong state and a strong society. (Ibid.).

In this relationship between competent strategic actors, relationships are formed in two ways. They can be the outcome of the communicative process between actors and planning (deliberate strategies) or be derived the from actions of relevant actors. These are ideal types. Planned or deliberate strategies presuppose control over the implementation of plans. This is equivalent to Etzioni's control over developmental trajectories. They do not allow the process of learning, equivalent to Etzioni's developmental consensus. Emergent strategies presuppose processes of social learning and exclude active control (Mintzberg, 1989: 32). Ideally, we tend towards a combination of both approaches, which allows learning and control over the implementation of strategy. This is the quality of developmental societies. Active societies are the best equipped to steer social changes in conditions of complexity. This is also a manifestation of the adaptive nature of modern social systems. An active society strongly emphasises the communicative aspect and seeks the complementarity of divergent interests.

Actors of strategic steering must take into account limitations coming from the environment. These can be quite 'objective' (e.g., coming from the natural environment) but they can also be social and cultural limitations. This includes interests of other strategic actors and many other institutional constraints and social structures. Hence, the process of strategic steering is not only a technocratic problem, but also – or above all – a social process.

---

9   Evans is aware that these linkages can lead to both constructive linking of interested actors, as well as to establishment of corruptive and rent-seeking behaviour (Evans, 1997: 180).

Strategy as a social process

On the basis of his research in strategic management, Henry Mintzberg (1998) developed a classification of various definitions of strategies. The first is *strategy as plan*. In this category are concepts that define strategy as an intentional plan or guidelines for action (blueprint). This approach focuses on two characteristics of strategies: they are intentional and purposeful, and they are formulated before the action itself (e.g., Drucker, 1974). The second category, *strategy as ploy*, is quite similar to the first and could perhaps even be classified as its subcategory. It is a specific manoeuvre to 'outwit' the opponent. These concepts are appropriate for dealing with competitive situations or negotiation processes (Porter, 1980). The third category, *strategy as pattern*, focuses on behaviour related to the formulation and implementation of a strategy. These definitions focus on a pattern in a stream of actions. The fourth category of definitions, *strategy as position*, deals with the relationship of a strategic actor (individual or collective) and its environment. Strategy is an 'intermediary' between the strategic actor and the environment (i.e., internal and external contexts) (Thompson, 1967). The fifth category of definitions, *strategy as perspective*, seeks to locate the organisation in external organisation. This approach depends on strategic actors' perspective of their environment. One such approach is Selznick's discussion of the 'character' of organisation (Selznick, 1957).

Differences in approaches, which focus on different aspects of strategic processes, point to the conclusion that strategic steering is not only a simple technocratic process. Instead, it consists of multi-layered and complex social processes. Strategic processes are social processes and while dealing with possibility of strategic steering of development, we also encounter some key sociological questions. One such question is the relationship between actor and structure (micro-macro in the American sociological tradition). In the framework of *strategy as plan* (also *strategy as ploy*) and *strategy as perspective* approaches, we can also ask about the possibility of intentional influence on social structure. The question of the relationship between actor and structure is most clearly emphasised in the framework of approaches that define strategy as an intermediary between internal and external environment. The *strategy as patter* approach, focusing on the sequence of strategic actions, points to the time dimensions of strategic interactions between actors' mutual influence and social structures. This is not only about other actors in term of dyadic relationships or their influence as a sum of individual influences but about actions of emergent entity.

While studying steering of social development, we must dedicate special attention to these questions and issues. Dealing with debates with ideological and disciplinarily burdens (e.g., should the state play the key role in steering social development or should it be left to markets?) is counterproductive as it diverts debates from some of the key questions about the formulation and implementation of strategy and strategic processes.

Dimensions of strategic process

Sociology has intensively dealt with social changes from its early beginnings. After all, it was formed as a science in response to intensive social changes more than one hundred years ago. Nevertheless, to date it has dealt more with non-intentional action and less with forms and consequences of intentional action. It seems that studying this form of action remained in the domain of economic science, primarily dealing with *homo economicus*. In the framework of sociology, intentional action remained in the domain of rational choice theory. Despite that, recently a sociological approach to the research of strategic processes started to develop, in which strategy can be analysed as a form of social practice. In this *strategy as practice approach*, some researchers have successfully applied more recent sociological theories of practice (Giddens, 1979; Giddens, 1984; Bourdieu, 1990; de Certeau, 1988) and started dealing with one of the basic sociological questions through analysis of strategic processes: relationships between actors and structures (European sociological tradition) or macro and micro levels (American sociological tradition).

At this point, we again encounter the aforementioned difference between the strategic steering of the organisation and the strategic steering of social development. The first started to deal with actor-structures through research on influences of environment on social actors. The other deals with research on the possibility of the influence of social subsystems or collective actors on developmental trajectories. Foundations were laid by Etzioni's concept of the active society (Etzioni, 1968: 393).

An interesting starting point for discussion on the actor-structure relationship is the theory of structuration proposed by Anthony Giddens. (1979, 1984), in which he rejected functionalist and structuralist approaches, which presupposed too great a social determination of human beings or actors. This was denounced even much before that by Dennis Wrong as an 'over socialised conception of man' (Wrong, 1961). Giddens understands social reality to be a constantly changing and fluid object of research. Society exists in interactions between actors. Therefore, he changes the static notion of structure to a more dynamic notion of structuration. 'The structural properties of social systems are both medium and outcome of the practices they recursively organize' (Giddens, 1984: 25). He terms this theorem 'duality of structure'. The driving force of structuration is individual and collective actors.

Margaret Archer (1988) argues in her 'theory of morphogenesis' that social systems are capable of radical restructuration. The source of these changes is individual and collective actors. There are complex exchanges between action and structures, which result in social changes; the formation of structures takes place in practical interaction. Unlike Giddens, Archer argues for the principle of 'analytical dualism', which should replace 'duality of structure'. This implies that there is a need to introduce an analytical distinction between action and structure. Specifically, emergent qualities, which characterise socio-cultural systems, imply discontinuity between initial interactions and their products: complex systems (Archer, 1988: 61).

These theories represent an important starting point to study strategy as a social process, because they deal with the possibility of individual and collective actors influencing the structures of social systems intentionally. However, neither Archer or Giddens developed an apparatus that would allow us to locate strategy or strategic processes in the context of social processes. If society exists in interactions between social actors, we must ask about where to find and analyse these processes. Is a strategic process as intentional action taking place in a relationship between people or perhaps at the individual level? Archer's theory invites similar questions. Both individual strategies and collective strategies, which are the result of communicative processes among various actors; must take a number of limitations posed by social structures into account.

Social becoming

Sztompka's theory of social processes, *social becoming*, is more appropriate to model dimensions and levels of strategic processes. He shapes his vision of social reality on the basis of two analytical dichotomies. First, he distinguishes between two levels of social reality: *individuality* (people as individuals or as members of specific collectivities, e.g., groups, associations, communities, movements etc.) and *totality* (abstract social wholes of superindividual sort, social reality *sui generis*). He does not interpret the social whole as a metaphysical entity but as a structure. Individuals are neither passive objects nor completely autonomous, but as bounded agents (bounded rationality) (Sztompka, 1993). Second, he distinguishes between two forms of social reality: *potentiality* (inherent tendencies, capacities, capabilities) and actuality (processes, transformations, activities, development etc.). Tab. 1 shows Sztompka's vision of social reality, developed on the basis of these two dichotomies. Actors (we could also call them 'strategic actors') are actualised through social action. Structure, which is the social context of the strategic process, is actualised in operation.

Tab. 1: Sztompka's image of social reality

	Potentiality	Actuality
Totality	Structure (social context of strategic process)	Operation (relevant social processes)
Individuality	Agent (strategic actor)	Action (decision)

Reworked after Sztompka, 1993: 214

Relevant structures, which represent social context of strategic process, have emergent qualities. This implies that the structure is not merely the sum of the qualities of individual agents. The same goes for operations (relevant social processes); although action is a component of operations, operations cannot be reduced to individual actions; they have new specific emergent qualities.

According to Sztompka, structures can have individual dynamics. This assertion is based on three principles. The first is *inertia*, implying that it is more likely that functioning (e.g., developmental trajectory) will continue in the same direction that experience a radical change in direction. This phenomenon is 'commitment'; specific organisations insist on the same strategy for various reasons, although relevant actors are aware that doing so does not provide optimal or even acceptable solutions. However, sometimes significant change in strategy takes place. One such case is Ireland, which changed a very unsuccessful strategy of self-sufficiency and import substitution in the 1950s and 1960s, after holding to it futilely for decades. One can also mention Germany, not being able to break the trap of rigid institutions of a welfare state for a long time (Esping-Andersen, 1996). The second principle is 'momentum'. This implies that once the process is in place and it achieves a certain level, it is almost impossible to stop it and return to its starting point. It is more likely that the process will continue and that actors will try to modify it. The third is the principle of 'sequences': phases of the operation contain patterns, which often cannot be altered.

However, actions performed by actors are not only realisations of social trends. Actors are autonomous in relation to operations of structure to a certain extent.

Unlike Giddens and Archer, who insist on 'duality of structure' and 'analytical dualism', which contributes to the aforementioned problem of location of strategy at individual or supra-individual levels, Sztompka introduces a third, intermediary level. It is located between levels of individuality and totality, and Sztompka claims that it is the only real substance of social reality, specific social tissue (Sztompka, 1993: 217). According to Sztompka, each social event or process, which is the building unit of society, represents a fusion of both levels. It is therefore difficult to differentiate them, even if only for analytical purposes. He terms this intermediary level *praxis*:

> Praxis is where operation and action meet; a dialectical synthesis of what is going on in a society and what people are doing. It represents the confluence of operating structures and acting agents, the combined product of the momentum of operation (at the level of totalities) and the course of action undertaken by societal members (at the level of individualities). In other words, it is doubly conditioned (constrained and facilitated): from above, by the phase of functioning reached by wider society; and from below, by the conduct of individuals and their groups. Bu tit is not reducible to either; with respect to both levels, of individualities and totalities, it is a new emergent quality.
>
> (Sztompka, 1993: 217)

Praxis is actuality; therefore, there is also potentiality, which Sztompka terms 'agency'. It is the area where structures and actors meet. It is also doubly conditioned and is the synthetic product of structural circumstances and capacities of individual and collective actors. However, as in the case of praxis, agency cannot be reduced to sum of qualities of actors or to expression of the environment. It is a new, emergent level.

Praxis and agency are connected. Just as an agent is mobilised in action and a structure is unfolding in operation, agency is 'eventuating' in praxis. Sztompka uses the notion of 'eventuation' to show that agency can agency be actualised as a social event, which is the basic unit of social reality in his theory. In the context of our research, this process is a strategic process. It is possible that potentiality is not eventuated. In this case, society does not realise its strategic potential.

However, this model is not sufficient, as it contains the idea of linear development, which is expressed in unidirectional linkages from potentialities to actualities. In reality, the level of actuality has a reverse impact on potentiality. Therefore, Sztompka introduces three feedback loops. First, on the level of totalities, redefinitions of structures take place, as a consequence of social operations, in 'structure-building' processes. Secondly, on the level of individuality, 'moulding of agents', as a consequence of agents' actions, takes place. Finally, on the intermediary level of social reality, 'agency-construction' takes place as a consequence of praxis (Sztompka, 1993: 218).

Sztompka developed his 'social becoming' approach as a generic model of social processes. In the context of this paper, however, we are interested in implications of this model to explain or model strategic steering of social development. Based on models of dimensions and levels of social process, we can design a model of dimensions and levels of strategic processes that includes our debate. On the level of individuality, the analysis focuses on strategic action of strategic actor as a potentiality. This can be both individual and collective actors. On the level of totality, there is a socio-cultural field, which includes social and cultural factors that limit the set of options for strategic actors. Sztompka uses the notion of the socio-cultural field to denote the multi-dimensionality of inter-individual 'social tissue'. Social tissue consists of four types of linkages, which are interpersonal, emergent in nature. He describes these dimensions by using INIO typologies: ideal (I), normative (N), interactive (I), and (O) opportunity. At the first level, a continuous formulation, legitimisation, and reformulation of ideas is taking place. At the normative level, continuous institutionalisation, reaffirmation or rejection of regulations, ethical codes, and similar is taking place. At the action level the continuous establishment, differentiation and reformulation of interactive channels and linkages at different levels occurs. At the interest level, there is continuous crystallisation, petrification, and redistribution of opportunities, interests, and similar. (Sztompka, 1934: 11). Ideal (ideal) and normative (rules) linkages contribute to culture. Interactions and interests contribute to social tissue (structures) (Sztompka, 1993: 10–11). The socio-cultural field is unfolding as developmental trajectory through emergent strategies.

At the intermediate level, which is, according to Sztompka's model of social processes, a level of social reality with the event as a basic unit of sociological analysis, we can locate (as a potentiality) strategic area, networks, and cognitive space. It is eventuating in strategic processes. The realised strategy is a result of emergent and planned strategy (Mintzberg, 1998: 36).

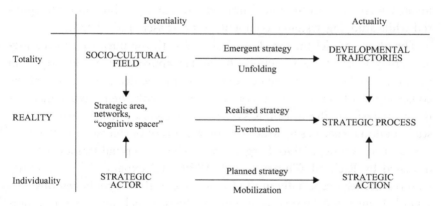

Fig. 1: Dimensions and levels of the strategic process

Actors, as seen in Fig. 1, can mobilise their capacities and resources in the form of strategic action. However, this is not the necessary outcome. In certain circumstances, these resources are not utilised in processes of the strategic steering of social development and remain a potentiality. The question of necessary conditions for effective utilisation of existing resources must be explored. This is not only a theoretical problem but a highly relevant one in the context of formulation of developmental policies. For example, do we have to invest new resources in the improvement of specific factors of development (e.g., increase R&D funding), or should we instead attempt to increase the efficiency of already existing inputs (e.g., by improving cooperation between R&D institutions and business sector)? This is a critical question because strategic action contributes to changes in the strategic capacities of actors, either through a virtuous circle or a vicious circle.

The socio-cultural field (in Fig. 1) represents a important element of the environment, limiting the options of strategic actors. Sztompka is discussing two types of environments: natural environment and social consciousness. In this paper, the aspect of natural environment is less important, although we cannot ignore it. However, the role of natural resources in competitiveness and the ability to steer social development is reduced (Porter, 1990: 4). Hence, we are focusing on that aspect of the environment, which we term 'socio-cultural environment', and it cannot be ignored while studying systemic competitiveness (Esser et al., 1996).

The above model (in Fig. 1) is designed with the purpose of sociological analysis of strategic action. A similar approach was developed in organisational sociology and economic geography, dealing with social the construction of enterprises in communication with their environment. It is an analysis of the 'business systems framework', which was used to study national specifics in structure and actions of businesses and the business sector (Whitley, 1996; Sorge, 1996). The conceptual framework was designed by Richard Whitley (1992, 1999) and expanded by Scandinavian researchers, especially in the framework of the Copenhagen business school. Unlike neoclassical economic analysis, which ignores the importance of history, institutional arrangements and collective actors, enterprises are understood as embedded in nationally and regionally specific institutional contexts. This context is a 'host' of certain types of economic organisations (inter- and intra-organisational forms and practices). Local economic and social institutions represent the broader environment, which determines sets of possibilities. Analysis of the business system focuses on the role of these arrangements in current and future actions as a part of the historic process. From the perspective of this study, their conceptualisation of the institutional context of the business system (i.e., its environment) is especially interesting. It is divided into *proximate social institutions* and *background social institutions*. The former are 'classical' economic institutions (financial systems, educational systems, the tradition of state interventionism, industrial relations, etc.). These institutions are also socially constructed; their functionality is relative and depends on the respective business system. The institutions are dominant beliefs, conventions, moral codes, and similar that lead interaction and cooperation. Here we are referring to the cultural aspects of the environment.

Starting from the general issues of rationality linked to the steering of societal development and considering (though very briefly) several relevant sociological theories, we have thus reached a comparatively feasible and more specific model that may contribute to the further understanding of the strategic steering of development.

Path-dependency and social development

Analysis of the strategic action of developmental latecomers shows that it is an issue that touches the very core of sociological analysis. It is, at the same time, an issue that definitely touches economic theory. This overlap is perhaps strongest in the framework of neo-institutional analysis, which deals with classical macro-sociological issues (i.e., emergence, preservations of institutions, institutional changes) and at the same time integrates economic and sociological approaches (Alvesson and Spicer, 2018; Nee and Brinton, 1998: xv). Furthermore, neo-institutional analysis in sociology is also important when studying strategic processes, as it deals with the idea of contextually dependent rational action. It focuses on socio-cultural contexts within the frame of which individual interests and cultural elements, important for determining the strategic actions of actors (culture as a tool kit, Ann Swidler), develop, as well as the reciprocal role of norms and interests in transformations of institutional environment.

Neo-institutional analysis in sociology attempts to explain strategic action as a type of action taking place in the context of incomplete information and mental models, which contributes to transaction costs. Strategic actors regularly deal with these conditions (Nee, 1998: 1). It is important to note that transaction costs are an important part of the costs of production and exchange in contemporary economies. Therefore, alternative institutional arrangements can be the difference between economic growth, stagnation, and recession (North, 1990; Nee, 1998) on a macro level. However on a micro level the institutional arrangement can lead to conflicts, especially when competition, or even cooperation between two actors is limited by rules (Shahab and Lades, 2021) and especially by complicated rules (Williamson, 1993). This is also valid in the case of strategic action of actors. The reciprocal action of strategic actors is connected with numerous potential costs. (This is expressed in situations like the prisoner's dilemma, etc.). Capacities for harmonious action between them can mean the difference between potentiality and actuality, which eventualises itself in the form of a successful strategic process. Analysis of factors that enable mobilisation, eventuation, and uncovering (i.e., the transformation of potentiality into actuality) is of key importance for the analysis of strategic processes, in the same way that the specification of conditions that encourage actors to form efficient institutional arrangements (North, 1990, also Shahab and Lades, 2021) is of key importance for explanation of economic growth (also Corradini, 2021).

The concept of *choice within constraints* is the theoretical centre of neo-institutional analysis. Networks of interrelated norms and regulations are formal and informal constraints, shaping the selection of options for the actors (Nee, 1998: 8). They can solve the problem of coordination and enable collective action. Norms are a type of social capital, enabling us to solve dilemmas and leading to optimal collective results. Suboptimal results occur when individual actors follow their specific strategic goals (goal rationality) and ignore rationality from the perspective of the system as a whole (systemic rationality). Norms of cooperation enable systemic discourse and systemic rationality.

One of the key questions is, as already mentioned, whether developmental trajectories can be influenced by strategic choices or whether development is 'path-dependent'. By adopting the 'choice within constraints' approach, neo-institutional analysis also adopts the 'path-dependency' approach to development. Regardless of the discipline, neo-institutional analysis has one common notion: 'path-dependency'. Douglass North, one of the most relevant neo-institutionalists, has developed an approach that is closer to the choice within constraints, in which social structures and culture do not determine but limit the set of options: on each step of the path there are choices, political and economic, which help to determine proper alternatives. 'Path-dependence' is a method of conceptual reducing available choices and not a story about an inevitable future (North, 1990).

> At every step along the way there were choices - political and economic - that provided real alternatives. Path dependence is a way to narrow conceptually the choice set and link decision making through time; it is not a story of inevitability in which the past neatly predicts the future.
>
> (North, 1990: 98–99)

Process is 'path-dependent' in cases in which the initial movement in one direction determines the future direction. The sequence of events influences new events in a way that developmental trajectories limit the set of options for future trajectories. Path dependence can also be triggered by contingent events that establish reinforcing patterns of actions and reactions (Rolland and Hanseth, 2019). This is consistent with two other phenomena. First, in chaotic systems, which also includes social (and economic) systems, there are positive feedback lops. These are self-reinforcing mechanisms that intensify social processes. Second, social structures usually have emergent quality and independent dynamics, which is manifested in principles of inertness and sequences.

The aforementioned definition of path-dependency leads to a specific methodological status of this approach. One must take into account that this is not a typical theory or model of development as it does not offer a general list of relevant variables, which could be utilised for 'diagnostic and prescriptive research' and does not offer hypotheses about generally valid causal links between these variables (Ostrom, 1999: 39). 'Path-dependency' is an empirical category, which can be utilised for the explanation of a specific type of process in the time dimension. This approach does not offer a generalised explanation about why systems sometimes develop in this way. Instead, researchers using this concept must develop their own explanatory frameworks, theories, and models to explain the foundations of path-dependent processes.

It follows from this that not every developmental trend or set of decisions can be understood with the help of the concept of path-dependency. Path dependence is best referred to as historical contingent events that impact present options for change (Rolland and Hanseth, 2019). Sociologists must be careful when using this explanation, as correlations between starting conditions, general lawfulness, and path-dependence must be taken into account. There is no single 'best' method of analysis for the explanation of specific developmental trends; the adequacy of a particular method depends on the phenomena that we wish to explain. The use of path-dependency explanation would be less adequate for the explanation of phenomena or trend that occurs frequently, but on the basis of various starting conditions. In this case, one would have to search for the explanation on the basis of theory of rational choice, which would lead to convergence of developmental trends. For the explanation of phenomena that occurs only sporadically, but on the basis of similar starting conditions, one should search for the solution in specific general lawfulness that connects certain starting conditions with certain results. With the help of path-dependence, we can explain a specific trend that occurred only once, despite the existence of similar starting conditions somewhere else. Of course, one must take into account the possibility of spreading by diffusion, for example the first industrial revolution that occurred as such only once and then spread further. As noted above, path dependence is best understood as a causal process influenced by early events and the early event is a contingent event, inevitably linked to environment that led to the early event (Rolland and Hanseth, 2019).

Neo-institutional analysis also focused, with the help of path-dependency explanations, on the question of what enables the survival of societies, economies, and institutional arrangements that operate sub-optimally or are ineffective. Douglas North is of the opinion that the reason for this is that institutions do not come into existence in the framework of zero transactional costs: 'But if the process by which we arrive at today's institutions is relevant and constrains future choices, then not only does history matter but persistent poor performance and long-run divergent patterns of development stem from a common source' (North, 1990: 93). In accordance with the evolutionary approach, ineffective institutions should perish in the process of selection on account of more effective ones. However, the institutional change is incremental and path dependent (North, 2005, Meijerink, 2011). Effective institutions make sure that self-reinforcement is in place by using the following mechanisms: initial set-up costs, organizational learning effects, difficulty to exit once the solution is reached, and path dependence (Meijerink, 2011). However, this is not so, which was proven decades ago, when modernisation and convergence developmental theories were falsified. This is the reason that we cannot regard certain ways as optimal from the aspect of assuring of development or expect that 'optimal' forms will be established through the process of selection. Attention must also be paid to the role of intentional action in the formation of institutional arrangements.

Path-shaping as a coordination through systemic discourse

Due to the 'choice within constraints' approach, the discussion of path-dependency includes 'path-shaping' dimensions. In his analysis of institutional reforms of the welfare state (undoubtedly a case of institutional arrangements for which it is difficult to achieve fast changes due to numerous vital and expensive interests), Jacob Torfing shows that changes in well-established arrangements are indeed taking place, but policymakers and other stakeholders have to take complex constellations of interests into account. He defined policy path as a relatively stable way to organise and regulate certain policy fields. Policy path is not just a policy-making method for the regulation of objects, processes, and actions. It is a discursive terrain on which objects of regulation, regulatory agencies, and institutional forms of regulation are mutually structuring (Torfing, 2001: 286–287). Similarly, Rolland and Hanseth (2019) discuss the possibility of institutional arrangements getting broken through the destabilizing assemblages that can occur when other sub-assemblages are being stabilized. They interpret the dynamics on the socio-technical field when analysing the process of digital transformation.

The formation of strategies thus unrolls in a complex interaction between intentional measures, long-term traditions, processes of learning, and random events. In this process, a more or less coherent whole emerges from different elements and this whole represents the reproduction of a particular path. As already mentioned, this path is not necessarily optimal from the aspect of reaching systemic rationality.

'Path-shaping' is therefore possible through coordination between individual actors, which leads to coordinated strategic action. In this way, the strategic process can have realistic possibilities for success. However, even in the case of successful coordination, total discontinuity is not possible. Old arrangements and structures exercise some influence on the new ones. 'Path-shaping' and 'path-dependency' are complementary notions. The first is based on the assumption of changes in existing institutional arrangements; the second is based on the inability to completely change. It is therefore not possible to discuss institutional vacuum even in such rapid social and institutional changes as the post-socialist transition.

Institutional design is a difficult process that faces many challenges (Gray, 2020). Offe specifically mentions two problems: "'hyper-rationality' and 'mental residuals'"(Offe, 1995). Therefore, two conditions must be met to achieve successful institutional design (Offe, 1995: 54–55). First, institutional arrangements must be discredited and without legitimacy and ability to deal with challenges that come from their environment. In the case of economic development. This could be the situation of a deep and lasting economic crisis, which cannot be solved in the framework of existing arrangements (e.g., aforementioned cases of Ireland). Second, they have to offer an alternative vision. Therefore, such models are usually not 'structured' in a specific social setting but are in their initial form imported from different and more successful ones. They are adapted to local circumstances. If these two conditions are not met, institutional reforms will most likely meet serious obstacles.

Too great effort to change institutional arrangements can lead to a lack of trust. Too radical and insufficiently defined reforms overestimate the trust of stakeholders, which is a key prerequisite for successful systemic discourse (Haček et al., 2013: 256). Alternatively, they tend to support great expectations regarding the success of reforms (Offe, 1995: 56), such as the myth of designer capitalism (Stark, 1995). The survival and success of new institutional arrangements depend primarily on the trust of people and their willingness to meet the costs related with transition to new institutional arrangements (Ibid: 57).

Cultural political economy and the EU[10]

In the first two chapters, I frequently discussed those 'intangible' influential factors: if working network forms of coordination will be established between actors; if certain potentialities will become actuality; if a strategic discourse that enables the influence of actors on structures, which otherwise would not be possible, will occur. I will continue this study with research on these factors, and in the following chapter I will focus on the Cultural Political Economy of the EU.

The European Union (EU) has been continuously rethinking its position in the globalised world mainly by attempting to formulate strategies to increase its competitiveness. However, the EU has a long record of a substantial policy implementation deficit (Makarovič and Rek, 2017). This is also generally recognised for the initially ambitious EU development strategy, commonly known as the Lisbon Strategy, which has been perceived as a relative disappointment. After the revisions of the strategy in 2005, this widespread impression has remained, and the new version of the strategy was developed under the title 'Europe 2020'. The causes of failure have been attributed to various factors, such as the lack of focus in setting the goals and inefficient governance structures.

The central purpose of this part is to test and demonstrate whether and how strategic steering can be considered a discursive practice influenced by semiotic and extra-semiotic factors, which implies that success or failure of strategy essentially depends on one's ability to steer the discourse. The implementation problems, however, do not necessarily affect the latent function of the Lisbon Strategy (and its further modifications), namely to contribute to the reproduction of the European Union as a self-referential social system through the discourse. It will be argued that it is not only the generation and implementation of the strategy that depends on the discourse but also the subject of strategic steering. The EU is not simply a 'naturally' given spatial object but a social system that reproduces itself as on-going communication.

---

10 This chapter is partly co-authored with Matej Makarovič and Janez Šušteršič.

The problems of macro level strategic steering can only be understood in broader theoretical framework considering some of the key features of the modern social systems, such as the EU. Its key features particularly relevant for our discussion are rationality and complexity. While high levels of rationalisation and reflection capacities are supposed to increase the strategic steering potentials, the latter are also clearly limited by the increasing societal complexity. Social systems, as presented, for instance, by Niklas Luhmann's social systems theory, can handle the enormous amounts of selections required in the context of high complexity only by increasing their functional differentiation. The situation is even more complex at the European supra-national level due to the significance of segmental differentiation, which remains particularly important for the functioning of the political system (particularly in the sense of nation-states, sub-, and supra-national regions) both as a potential and an obstacle for the strategic steering.

Strategic solutions at the macro level can only be found in the directions of sophisticated contextual steering instead of any direct and centralised interventions. We are looking for the analytical and practical solutions to the problem of steering in a complex social setting in evolutionary mechanisms of the variation, selection, and retention of strategic discourses. These mechanisms are notably formulated in the 'cultural political economy' approach, a theory that provides us with the tools to analyse the shaping of strategic discourse by applying semiotic and extra-semiotic mechanisms.

Finally, we intend to analyse the EU strategic documents ranging from the Lisbon Strategy to Europe 2020 from the aspects of discourse and differentiation and present their failure to start functioning as successful economic imaginaries at the European and national levels.

It may be argued that the potentials and problems with the creations and implementations of strategies at the European Union level may be related to the relationship between the two aspects and their limitations, namely rationality and complexity. While rationality makes strategies at the macro level possible, complexity may have the opposite effect, though the factual relationship between them may be somewhat more sophisticated. To demonstrate this, we need to elucidate some basic points about the features, limits, and mutual relationship of both rationality and complexity to explain their impact on the EU's (in)ability to generate and implement viable strategies.

The features of modern social systems: Rationality and complexity

For Max Weber, rationality was a key feature of Western modernity (Weber, 1905/1992) with the superior steering potentials of bureaucratic organisations and the potentials of modern rational-legal state authority based on the rule of law and representative democracy. The increasing rationality of modern societies has also been seen as a way for societal steering at the macro level towards a better society. An early sociological manifestation of these views can be found in the works of Lester Ward, whose evolutionary theory focuses on the shift from the earlier historical stage of spontaneous societal evolution called 'the genesis' to the stage of telesis or the human-led societal evolution. Beck, Giddens, and Lash address a similar issue under the concept of reflexive modernisation, emphasising the ability of late modern societies to reflect on their own modernisation and respond to these reflections (Beck et al., 1994).

However, the Weberian concept of rationalisation and its application at the macro level in order to generate and implement societal strategies have not turned out to be necessarily compatible. Weber himself clearly noted that the rational behaviour of individuals generates emergent social phenomena with the life of their own, forming the 'iron cage'. Similarly, his contemporary Georg Simmel emphasised the growing tendency of human social and cultural creations to start the life of their own as more-than-life. Moreover, many individual rational actions within market economies and the representative democracies generate 'collective intelligence' (Willke, 2009: 125–126), whose results may be quite different from the expectations and desires of many or sometimes even most of the participating individuals.

For a classical account on the limits of rationality, one may refer to Herbert Simon and his concept of bounded rationality. He claims that even supposedly rational actors, either individual or collective, are unable to generate optimal solutions; instead, they have to find a solution that they see as the best within the limited understanding of the existing reality and the even more limited chances of predicting the actual outcomes of their actions. The concept of bounded rationality implies that market-based choices are far from optimal since they are not based on reality but only on an actor's perception of reality. However, the rationality of the decision makers at the macro level is (at least) equally bounded, while the consequences of their (misjudged) decisions may be even more significant. Following Simon, the limited rationality among the policy makers emphasising 'the incremental, random, non-rational, and sub-optimized nature of public governance' (Duit et al., 2010: 367) was described by Charles Lindblom.

The limits of rationality have also been considered by Amitai Etzioni (1968). His ideal active society is supposed to combine superior intentional steering mechanisms with the strong mechanisms of authentic consensus-building. Being aware that actors' choices can hardly be fully rational, Etzioni proposes a mixed-scanning approach that gets closer to 'muddling through' policies in the sense of Lindblom (1959) in everyday issues while attempting to build and implement consensus only concerning the most strategic issues.

The concerns of Simon, Lindblom, and Etzioni are in fact related to the issue of complexity. It may be argued that it is the relative amount of complexity compared to the abilities of the 'rational' actors (or controlling/steering systems) that prevent the optimal choices. Complex systems are inevitably only partially identifiable, only partially observable, and only partially controllable. For the purposes of this book, we are limited to aggregate complexity, implying particular relationships between systems' components. In this sense, complex systems exist in a (co-evolutionary) relationship to their environments, and are characterised by emergent qualities, learning capacities, and self-organization, as well as circular causality and irreversibility related to path-dependence. Within this framework, we can refer to Niklas Luhmann's claim that a system should be called complex when, because of the number and/or features of the system's elements, each element cannot be related to each other element at the same time (Luhmann, 1995). Complexity thus provides a wide variety of options among which selections are required; it generates both the opportunities given by the variety of options and the threats of selecting the wrong ones.

Rational strategic steering may have ambivalent impact on systems complexity. By strategically reducing the possible options, complexity may decrease. In contrast, the existence of elaborated plans as the description of the system within the system generates new complexity, even changing the very parameters on which the strategy has been based (see: Luhmann, 1995). Moreover, following Ashby's law of requisite variety, complexity can only be dealt with by complexity since the steering mechanism should be complex enough to foresee and properly respond to the complex systems features. This does not mean, however, that complexity may increase indefinitely without running into certain limits. Increasing complexity comes with a price and may lead to diminished returns.

It should be added that at least a partial but a very common solution of this problem lies in differentiation that distributes the potentials and burdens of complexity between new, smaller units. The result of differentiation is that nobody has to deal with the entire complexity but only with certain aspects and segments of it, while new type of complexity may emerge at the level of interrelations between the newly differentiated units that often needs to be coordinated. Differentiation thus deals with complexity by placing it at another level. Historically, the most typical differentiation was segmental based on the co-existence of mutually similar and relatively self-sufficient units (e.g., clans, tribes, empires, ethnicities, nations), while a typical trend of modernisation is the growth of functional differentiation based on different, highly interdependent, specialised units. This distinction is based on the classical contribution by Emile Durkheim on mechanical and organic solidarity, while the concept of functional differentiation has the long-established tradition in the 19th-century evolutionism by Herbert Spencer, Weber's autonomous social orders, Parsons' structural functionalism, Bourdieu's semi-autonomous social fields, and Niklas Luhmann's social systems theory, which is taken here as the major point of departure.

EU as a complex social system

Since a societal evolution tends to be characterized (among other aspects) by the growth of complexity, rhe European Union as the emergent entity composed by some of the world's most modern societies is an extremely complex social system, demonstrating high levels of functional and segmental differentiation.

Luhmann's social systems theory provides a good analytical starting point since it reaches beyond the old concept of society, typical for classical sociology and geopolitics, in which 'society' has been understood strictly as a political societies represented by a nation-states (Kessler and Helmig, 2007). From this traditional perspective, the EU can either be understood as a union of states-societies or as a new super-society. From the aspect of Luhmann's social systems theory, it is neither of these. For Luhmann, the concept of society as such is not based on political organization and/or other aspects of integration but simply on communication as its only constitutive element, which enables the society to reproduce itself in an autopoietic sense, producing communication by communication (Luhmann, 1995). Luhmann thus takes the single world society as his starting point – as the sum of all communication. Neither the EU nor its Member States can thus be considered societies according to Luhmann but only segmentally organised subsystems of the world society. The borders between these subsystems can only exist through communication, as the only material they are made of. Nation-states and the European Union thus exist to the extent that they are communicated. Mutually overlapping combinations of localities, nation-states, sub- and supra-national as well as macro-regions may thus coexist through compatible or competitive discourses.

This constructivist nature of social systems, however, does not imply the ability that they can be readily changed and reconstructed by some simple voluntarist actions. On the contrary, autopoietic self-referential systems are operationally closed, according to Luhmann, developing the principles of their own. They cannot be readily re-formed from their environments following some expectations from the 'outside', for they are in fact the ones that construct their perceptions of their respective environments in their particular way. Intervening to the auto-poetic self-referential social systems may thus produce the effects very different from the expected ones.

According to Luhmann, the modern (world) society is increasingly differentiated into functional subsystems, such as the economy, politics, science, intimate relations, law, religion, education, among others. While strongly interdependent because of their specialised nature, they are also increasingly autonomous and based on their specific internal principles. Social systems theory thus abandons the old functionalist notion of stability based on value and normative consensus since no super-system of values can exist above all the other systems in a differentiated de-centric society. Consequently, Willke (2009) claims there may be no more single morality above the world of differentiated subsystems. Instead, one should rely on the formal-legal (democratic) procedures that replace any value-normative content by increasingly cognitive decision making. It may be added that in the same manner that a single morality is becoming impossible: one can also hardly speak of any single central rationality. What is rational for economy is not necessarily rational for science and what is rational for science is not necessarily rational for politics. Any kind of macro-strategy should take this into account.

This does not necessarily imply that the social systems should be left at the macro level to the blind evolution, as implied by Luhmann (1995). To overcome the lock-in problems (Vasileiadou and Safarzyńska, 2010) and the potentially destructive effects of particular subsystems appreciating only their own perspective, one cannot rely solely on spontaneous order. While order may be for free, since some kind of order forms by itself, the desired order is not. 'Investment' into sophisticated models of coordination between the differentiated systems taking into account their particular principles, strengthening their reflexion abilities, and intervening in highly contextualized terms (Willke, 1995) thus seems to be a necessity.

We should add that the situation is even more complicated as claimed by Luhmann who tends to project the relevance of segmental subsystems into the past, emphasising only the functional differentiation of modern society. We argue instead, while acknowledging the increasing primacy of functional differentiation, that segmental divisions remain significant and should also be taken into account. Speaking of the global world society, these divisions become even more visible and obvious. Clearly, they are dynamic, unstable, and overlapping but they do exist, and they do have their own particular logics. It may be argued that the self-referential operations of the segmental systems are based on the concept of belonging (in the sense of an 'us'/'them' distinction). However, to remain consistent with Luhmann's social theory, belonging should not be understood as the people being a part of the social system (since the latter only consists of auto-poetically self-reproduced communication) but as continuously communicating the belonging issue. One should not understand belonging to the system in a literal sense as a person and organism being a part of a system but as communicating the belonging (Makarovič and Rončević, 2010: 26) to a nation-state, a region, an ethnicity, and similar.

In the case of the European Union, we are thus dealing with functional boundaries that 'are orthogonal to territorial boundaries' (Kessler and Helmig, 2007: 578). Strategy at the European level thus requires the sophisticated coordination of both aspects, which may be particularly difficult when the spatial perception of different subsystems does not overlap, meaning that different functional subsystems do not perceive segmental divisions in the same way. These inconsistencies, particularly between the spatial perceptions of the economy, politics and education, contributed, according to Kessler and Helmig (2007), to the failure in the implementation of the Lisbon Strategy. We assume that some additional understanding of the Lisbon Strategy and its implementation problems may also be found in the discursive logics of both the European Union and its strategy-building capacities.

Managing complexity through discourse steering

Since European Union is continuously (re)produced through communication processes, the discourses themselves are a major part of the EU operations. From the perspective of social systems theory, it can also be argued that discourse management is one of the key tools for encouraging reflexion, contextual intervention, and systems discourse (Willke, 1995). One could even hypothesise that discourse management is perhaps the only way of management in the 'multi-scalar governance' of the EU (Jessop, 2008). We could say that the Lisbon Strategy is perhaps a very useful indication of strategic processes in the EU. Jessop (2008: 208) claims that the Lisbon Strategy and the White Paper on governance are the latest phase of the search for appropriate forms of meta-governance at the EU level.

The policymaking at the EU level is indeed extremely complex and is in itself a very good example of the hyper-complex nature of contemporary social systems, in which continuously repeated attempts towards complexity reduction themselves contribute to ever-increasing complexity.

When discussing the EU, we should not only take the core EU apparatus but follow the strategic-relational approach and include the ever growing ensemble of all relevant actors into our analysis: 'EU policies are evolving in a larger framework of agenda-setting and policy-making by international institutions, supranational apparatuses, intergovernmental organizations and forums transnational think tanks, and transnational interest groups and social movements' (Jessop, 2008: 216). Despite the oft-claimed lack of legitimacy of the EU, it is quite obvious that it does not exist in isolation from other actors but is embedded in a wider political system at multiple levels; in fact, the EU structure is designed to accommodate this.

Here, we can turn to Jessop's cultural political economy, distinctive post-disciplinary approach to the analysis of social formations, including the EU with its formal institutional structures and complex multi-level governance structures and discourses, both formal and informal. The cultural political economy seems especially useful here for a variety of reasons. First, it builds on the well-known general evolutionary mechanisms of variation, selection, and retention, which are also present in some advanced variants of social systems theory. Second, this approach applies evolutionary mechanisms in the analysis of path-dependent and path-creative semiotic and extra-semiotic aspects of political and economic systems (i.e., actually existing economies). Finally, it allows us to conceptualise and analyse the path-shaping potential of strategic documents and practices, hence also the Lisbon Strategy. Therefore, by applying its conceptual apparatus, we can diagnose the causes for the relative failure of the EU's most recent attempt to become the most competitive economy.

According to Jessop and Oosterlynck (2008), economic imaginaries have a crucial constitutive role in the creation of existing economies. The economic imaginary is a semiotic order: a specific configuration of genres, discourses and styles and, as such, constitutes the semiotic moment of a network of social practices in a given social field, institutional order, or wider social formation (Fairclough, 2003). The Lisbon Strategy is a typical economic imaginary. Successful economic imaginaries have their own constitutive force in the social, political, institutional, and material world. A very good example is the imaginary 'knowledge society' in Scandinavian countries. Specifically, they can identify, privilege, and stabilise some forms of political, economic and cognitive action over others.

However, why is it relatively difficult to introduce new economic imaginaries? The strategic process must go through five different mechanisms, as developed by Fairclough (2003) and Jessop and Oosterlynck (2008). First, there is continuing variation in discourses and practices. With every challenge, crisis and opportunity new discourses are proposed. Very few succeed; many fail. However, this is not a market type of competition. The second mechanism is the selection of specific discourses. Some are privileged, while others are not. Some are even overtly disapproved. Some discourses resonate in broader debates, while others echo away without being noticed by a larger and relevant audience. Not only semiotic but also material factors can play a role here. The third mechanism is the retention of some resonant discourses. This implies that they are included in actors' habitus, hexis, and personal identity. They can become part of organisational routines, become part of the official and unofficial rules, are objectified in the built environment, and similar. The fourth mechanism is reinforcement, through which some planned mechanisms some discourses can be privileged and others can be filtered out. Mechanisms can be both semiotic and material. Finally, there is the mechanism of selective recruitment, inculcation and retention by relevant social groups, organizations, institutions, and similar entities.

Discourse and differentiation in the EU strategic documents

Although the Lisbon Strategy was obviously favoured, becoming the official strategic document of the EU and its Member States, the distinction between planned and emergent strategy is indeed substantial but also with significant differences in implementation between the Member States themselves.

We can distinguish between the three distinctive periods in the creation and implementation of European strategic documents. The first started in 2000, when the initial Lisbon Strategy was adopted. Although originally planned with a ten-year time horizon, broad disappointment with the results led to refurbishing and re-launching the strategy in 2005. This began the second period. The third and the last one thus far started in 2010 with a new comprehensive strategy known as 'Europe 2020'.

Our account of these three periods is based on the official wording of the strategies as adopted at the highest political level, by each year's EU Council conclusions. Heads of States and Governments meet every March to discuss, among other issues, the progress in implementing the Union's development strategy. Almost every year they add some new priorities and targets, and in some years, as noted above, they may also comprehensively refurbish the strategy.

Council conclusions reflect the highest political agreement on priorities and implementation structure of the strategy. As such, these documents are rather diplomatic in wording and require scrutiny and comparison to understand the subtle but important variations in emphasis and content. Our purpose is to use these documents to analyse the characteristics of the strategic steering of development policies at the EU level. Our discussion is organised along the lines set out above. We present the changes in the level of functional differentiation and segmentation as well as the developments in the political discourse about the Lisbon Strategy.

To assess the level of functional differentiation, we examine the broadness of goals and functional policy areas included in each period's strategy. More importantly, we also assess whether there was an ambition to integrate different functional areas under one comprehensive approach, or whether, alternatively, functional areas were left to follow their own internal logic while constraining each other at the margin.

The original Lisbon Strategy of 2000 set the famous goal for Europe 'to become the most competitive and dynamic knowledge-based economy in the world, capable of sustainable economic growth with more and better jobs and greater social cohesion' (Council of the EU, 2000). Such goal-setting reflected the idea of Lisbon Strategy being the highest strategic document for fostering sustainable development, understood as a balance among economic, social, and environmental dimensions. Accordingly, the document covered many policy areas: information society, research and innovation, business environment, internal market, financial market, macroeconomic policy, education and training, employment, social protection, and social inclusion. Goals and targets were set for all these areas at the 2000 and subsequent spring council meetings. Grouping many policy areas and targets into one overall document, attempting to integrate them into one comprehensive and balanced approach, reflects a low level of functional differentiation in strategic steering.

The 2005 European Council recognised this comprehensiveness to be among the main reasons for the disappointing implementation. It 'refocused' the strategy on only two priorities, namely economic growth and employment, and 're-launched' it under the label of 'Growth and Jobs Strategy' (Council of the EU, 2005). While still paying lip service to the broad concept of sustainable development, it also narrowed the number of policy areas to knowledge and innovation, investment and work conditions, and growth and employment (Majetić et al., 2019). Many important areas, such as social inclusion and environmental sustainability, were addressed chiefly from the economic point of view and were expected to be dealt with in more detail by other strategic processes at the EU level. This reflects a conscious decision to increase the level of functional differentiation in strategic steering, whereby each functional area (economy, social development, sustainable issues, etc.) is addressed by specific strategies, while each of these sets marginal conditions for the others. For example, the economic strategy puts emphasis on research and development, but selection of priorities areas also includes technologies important for sustainable development.

In 2010, growth and employment were also made catchwords of the new strategy for the next decade, but a strong effort was made to integrate them more fully with issues such as climate change, energy sources, education, social inclusion, and territorial cohesion. The underlying integrating force between all these issues was expected to lie in innovation, technological progress and knowledge, as the basis both for increasing European global competitiveness and addressing the social and environmental concerns at the same time. The third period, therefore, is a move back to less functional differentiation. In contrast with Lisbon 2000, which aimed at integrating different areas in a balanced way, the most recent strategy looks for a small number of integrating issues, such as knowledge and innovation.

To assess the level of segmental differentiation, we discuss the changes in the so-called governance of the Lisbon Strategy. The basic problem for any kind of European-level strategic steering is that many important policies are left to the discretion of Member States. To deal with this issue, the

EU Council in 2000 invented the so-called Open Method of Coordination (OMC). It is a rather controversial approach to governance. On the one hand, Council Conclusions (Council of the EU 2000) stress that it should be 'a fully decentralized approach', used 'as the means of spreading best practice and achieving greater convergence towards the main EU goals'. This presents the OMC as a voluntary process of mutual learning and working together for the same goal. On the other hand, the conclusions opened the door to setting 'quantitative and qualitative indicators and benchmarks against the best in the world', thereby 'translating European guidelines into national and regional policies by setting specific targets and adopting measures', as well as for 'periodic monitoring, evaluation and peer review organized as mutual learning processes'.

During the years to follow, the European Commission tried to develop a common set of structural indicators for measuring countries' progress towards Lisbon goals. It also used the peer review process to informally monitor Member States' policies and to formulate proposals for country-specific policy recommendations to be adopted by the Council in the framework of Broad Economic Policy Guidelines. This meant that what on paper should be a truly decentralised learning process was gradually transformed into a process of a centrally coordinated monitoring exercise. Therefore, we classify this period as one of low segmentation in strategic steering.

Such an approach increasingly became a matter of criticism from influential Member States. It was stressed that any comparisons on the basis of a set of indicators are inherently incomplete and neglect differences in national preferences for (economic) policy outcomes. The implicit role of the commission as headmaster was seen as inappropriate.

To deal with these issues, the mid-term review of the Lisbon Strategy in 2005 introduced the concept of national ownership. This meant that all Member States should prepare their own National Reform Programs, on the basis of common guidelines but amended to local situations, discussed and possibly endorsed by a wide array of national stakeholders. Member States were also required to report on program's implementation every year.

Stressing the role of the national political process and ownership meant a move towards a more segmented steering approach. There were also no major changes to this approach by the 2010 Council.

The discourse of the first period, to some extent, reflected an ambitious idea to cover a wide variety of functional subsystems based on established common principles for both functional and segmental units. The catchwords of competitiveness and sustainability seemed to be suitable for this task. The second period brought forward a clear shift in the discourse, which become more strictly focused on the economic issues of growth and jobs, while also appreciating the existing segmental differentiation (the 'national ownership' concept). The third period discourse again tried to catch a variety of functional areas by a few key concepts such as knowledge and sustainability.

Clear shifts in both differentiation and segmentation dimensions can be noted. We have shown that such changes were introduced as a reaction to perceived weaknesses of existing approaches. This indicates that there is some flexibility in European strategic steering.

It seems that the low differentiation–low segmentation mix (Period 1) was inferior, as would also be predicted by our theoretical considerations of strategic steering in complex situations. It is, however, hard to say whether high segmentation is better combined with high differentiation (Period 2) or a low one (Period 3), since they were implemented in very different economic environments (i.e. booming economy vs. economic crisis).

Communication and education as a tool for implementation of grand strategies

The shifts in the developmental discourses, repetitive adjustments of the EU grand strategies and their implementation deficit clearly indicate that strategic steering of the European Union is not a straightforward, but a rather difficult and lengthy process, often resembling trial-and-error learning. Is this a consequence of the failure of policymakers to grasp the increasing functional and segmental differentiation of the European Union? Or is it a consequence of the fact that the Lisbon Strategy was immensely ambitious, underestimating the complexity of the EU itself?

In any case, the idea of the first version of the Lisbon Strategy was based on the flawed assumption that functional and segmental divisions of the European social system could be relatively easily overcome by clear common principles supposed to be represented by the discourse the strategy had put forward. This mistake was soon recognized by the EU as the Strategy was refocused half-way through its planned duration. After 2005 its newly adopted economic focus took into account the functional and segmental differentiation of the EU but to no avail. This approach failed as well but it is nevertheless surprising that the new adjustment, leading to the Europe 2020 strategy, returned to the initial positions of engaging a wider variety of fields, through the discourse emphasizing knowledge and sustainability as general principles, while considering the national (segmental) differences.

On the positive side, one could argue that the shift in focus and approach in 2005 and 2010 demonstrate the flexibility of the EU decision making process and its ability to realistically reflect the results of their actions, as well as its ability to propose new and different approaches. However, these shifts could not prevent the failure of the Lisbon Strategy. Furthermore, this casts a doubt on the implementation of the current Europe 2020 document. This is even more relevant given the gloomy prospects of the current financial and economic situation of the European Union and its staggering competitiveness as compared to the newly emerging centres of economic growth, especially in Asia.

We must emphasize that its failure is not due to the changed economic circumstances that could not have been foreseen when the initial document was adopted. Namely, the failure was quite evident and the first changes to the Lisbon Strategy were conducted well before the current economic and financial crisis. The main reason for the failure is the fact that it failed to establish itself as a hegemonic economic imaginary throughout the European Union, its Member States and sub-national units. It failed to progress through all five evolutionary stages as described by Fairclough (2003) and Jessop and Oosterlynck (2008) but has only passed through the first two instead. The Lisbon Strategy was produced as a relatively new and original discourse (variation) and was selected by the decision makers (the European Council, other EU institutions, and the national governments) as a privileged discourse resonating in a variety of relevant debates reaching a wide variety of relevant audiences, all the while being supported in semiotic and also in material ways (it was the basis for the EU financial mechanism, privileging certain types of projects over the others). However, it never reached the level of retention, as we cannot find evidence that it became a part of individual's habitus through general population. Hence, it also failed to become a part of organisational routines and a variety of official and unofficial rules. Consequently, it could also not be reinforced and recruited by all the most relevant groups, organisations, and institutions.

However, we cannot claim that the Lisbon Strategy was a complete failure. First, it was a part of the valuable collective learning process, pointing to dimensions which can be steered and where it is impossible to do so. It contributed to our knowledge about the mechanisms of the EU steering, and their potentials and limitations. We have also learned that the EU is becoming a hyper-complex social system, with a unique interplay of segmental and functional differentiation. Consequently, the intentional creation, selection, retention, reinforcement and recruitment of new economic imaginaries proved to be an extremely difficult task.

Second, this experience proved that the European Union can be relatively flexible despite its complexity. Consequently, recurrent crises can serve as an additional stimulus to increase the European integration. Interestingly, the European strategic failures as well as the recent global economic crisis have not led to national protectionism and disintegration but to the search for new common strategies (cf. Jones et al., 2010). Another such example is the EU response to public debt problems in several of its Member States.

Finally, communicating the Lisbon Strategy has been a process of communicating the European Union itself. Local communities, nation-states and sub- and supranational entities are not some pre-given 'natural' entities; they are social systems produced and reproduced through communication. The European Union is no exception to this general rule. It exists as it is communicated, and it only exists in communication. Hence, the EU grand strategies are not only more or less successful economic imaginaries with a constituting role in the material world but also the tools applied to continuously (re)constitute the European Union itself. This provides one obvious mechanism for improved implementation of grand strategic documents: education. We tested this educational approach as a part of Jean Monnet Chair action *Cultural Political Economy of Europe 2020* and demonstrated that, if used properly, it can be an effective mechanism for making them part of personal habitus and, consequently, of organisational routines (Rončević, 2019). The first education changes were tested through the online experience in times of COVID-19 restrictions (see also Getova and Mileva, 2021) where the digital divide became increasingly more important in disabling access to education. This holds especially true for developing countries (Singh and Singh, 2021). On the other hand, usage of ICT as a tool for education is not problematic; however, the excessive usage of ICT can become such (Macur, 2021). In this regard, the educational processes need to be planned and steered carefully and thoughtfully.

Conclusion

In line with the discussion, the successful implementation of strategic documents, such as the Lisbon Strategy, Europe 2020 and also Agenda 2030 could be operationalised as developmental steering. This steering occurs on the basis of these strategies, about which the social consensus was reached and whose implementation is carefully controlled through various mechanisms, such as the Smart Specialisation Strategies.

Our point of departure was the ascertainment of the complex nature of the economy and society. Reality doesn't confirm implicit, simplified assumptions (about simple structure, simple causal relationships, complete information, consensus about goals, resources and instruments, etc.), which appear within the framework of modern orthodox economic science and within the framework of 'state-centred' theories of developmental steering. The economy is – just like the other social systems – a chaotic system. Because of the mechanisms of the positive feedback loop, this limits the possibilities of successful hierarchical intervention.

The growing complexity of modern societies is mostly a consequence of their processes of differentiation; here Luhmann and Wilke primarily discuss functional differentiation, which causes the formation of specialized partial (sub)systems, which are autonomous in performing their function but which simultaneously lose the possibility of performing other functions. This also implies that the political system lost the possibility of autonomous steering of development. This explains why so much emphasis is put on stakeholder engagement at all levels, from local to supranational. Strategic processes are in the joint domain of all relevant systems or actors. They must use more refined mechanisms of steering; here, Wilke stresses reflexion (observing one's own impacts on the environment), contextual intervention (one indirectly impacts on the actions of other systems, by changing contextual conditions) and systemic discourse (searching for divergent interests by communication within the frame of negotiating arrangements).

Nevertheless, these mechanisms activate themselves primarily in more developed and democratic societies, where preconditions for systemic discourse are in place.

Our debate demonstrated that implementation of grand strategies demands transformation of strategic processes, change of relations between various partial systems and change in the nature of policies. Partial systems will have to develop capacities that will enable reflexion and the most sophisticated forms of communication. This, of course, means that partial systems and collective actors will have to use the mechanism of contextual intervention in their attempts at strategic steering. Developmental consensus will be reached on the basis of systemic discourse. Without it, it will, in the middle- to long-term, come to exhaustion of developmental potentials of innovation competitiveness and to stagnation[11].

These conclusions have significant implications for the research and practice of developmental steering, primarily for the comprehension of the role of the state, but also of supranational associations such as the European Union, in conditions of contextual differentiation and complex environment, which hinder or even disable classical mechanisms of hierarchical intervention. However some theses about its waning role are not correct. Even though the developmental success of highly developed countries depends on increasingly intangible factors, the role of the state is consequently even more important and the quality of its institutions even more essential than in the case of omnipresent but (because of low competency) weak state. In conditions of globalisation, the state can preserve its influence only if it acts as a relevant link in the network of actors. Power constellations in these networks are such that none of the actors can actually execute absolute power. However, within the frame of the network, the state is the one that could execute significant influence as a generator of impulses for systemic discourse, in which bearers of strategic

---

11 Singapore represents a partial exception. In that country, even economic development did not lead to distinctive internal communication. However, a more detailed analysis reveals the existence of intensive communications between politics and certain segments of the economy. Whether China will be the second exception will be clear when it makes the transition from a middle-income to a high-income society.

competencies participate in negotiating mechanisms of steering. Reflexion must, of course, come from all involved sides. Enterprises and other actors on the mezzo level thus must be capable of reflexion and self-reflexion.

In conditions of radical technological and organizational changes, the state faces new challenges. It will not be possible for it to avoid the role of initiator, coordinator, and stimulator. The promotion of short-term interest is one of the key dangers of networks, in which actors with partially limited strategic competencies participate. That is why the state will have to especially ensure that developmental processes will be based on middle- and long-term perspectives. The European Union is doing so through its grand strategies. However, active and anticipatory structural policy, initiated by the state, in no way means that indicative plans will be sketched by European, national, or regional agencies with limited knowledge. It would be unrealistic to expect something like this in the frame of heterarchical networks. The making of developmental strategies must be based on 'substantial dialogue', in which relevant actors participate and, in this way, they become key elements of the concept of directed economic and societal change.

Governments on various levels can indeed do much. They can foster mutual trust and social capital through their actions and can act as role models to other stakeholders (see Kukovič, 2022: 11–12). For example, by including them in a meaningful way in policy consultations so that they can assume the ownership of strategic processes. The cooperation of strong and competent public institutions and other stakeholders can be a powerful tool for development.

In the case of semi-peripheral East and South European societies, because of the weakness of many actors, the next question is also important: to what degree is the state capable of conversion from generator of strategic directives to generator of impulses for a-centric approach to strategy-making, meaning to what degree is the state capable of that, which Willke calls "'civilizing the powe'" (Willke, 1993)? This is about the transition from classical hierarchical intervention to contextual intervention, in the frame of which the state takes into account specific logics of action of other subsystems and attempts to steer them by interventions into their environment. This is the first step to the achievement of synergy. Measures for stimulation of social structures must become the key aspect of developmental strategies. These strategies must be directed to the mezzo- and meta-levels. The capacity for fostering associational behaviour is one of the most important components of the recipe for successful corporate strategies and more efficient public policies. The acceleration of social structures must become an integral part of developmental strategies.

In doing this, it must be taken into account that certain social structures are not *a priori* more suitable than others. The enforcement of networks as a method of social coordination does not mean that other forms are not important. In modern societies, numerous forms of coordination co-exist and interact. It is not about the dilemma of hierarchies v. networks *per se* that is crucial but how these forms operate in regard to the nature of product market, the extent of technological changes, the existence of the economies of scale, and similar issues. Considering these environmental conditions, the key question is not an organisation's form but its capacity for the creation and maintenance of robust architecture for producing and using knowledge from a wide range of resources (i.e., its association capacity). In this regard, there are no overly sharp differences between hierarchies and networks, because hierarchies are embedded in a wide range of inter-organisational networks.

From this perspective, attempts at stimulating faster development of East-European societies by the rapid implementation of free markets and parliamentary democracy revealed the incomprehension of the genesis of social systems, strategic processes, and dynamics of post-socialist societies. In this sense, two assumptions are especially erroneous. First, the fact that capitalist systems in developed societies did not come into existence over the night was neglected. Karl Polany described this process in his work 'The Great Transformation' (2001[1944]). His description of the development of capitalist systems in West Europe encompasses the period from the end of the 18th century to the second half of the 20th century, when he wrote his book. To this, one must add a very dynamic period of the last half of the century, in which, after all, the information-communication industrial revolution occurred. The capitalist system in the West had thus structured itself for more than two centuries. In this sense, the policies of economic development, which in stimulation of modernisation processes rely mainly on strengthening of the markets and diminishing the role of the state, often underestimate the weakness of markets and enterprises as well as the weakness and low capacities of the omnipresent state (Messner, 2013: 33). High costs, inefficiencies, and slowness in the implementation of market mechanisms and parliamentary democracy in the transitional countries of East Europe (and in some cases, the complete failure of such policies) are typical examples. It thus comes as no surprise that countries with better starting positions at the beginning of post-socialist transformation more easily faced the challenges at hand. In these countries, the capacities of actors for participation in processes of strategic steering were more developed. These are the capacities of learning, social organisation and integration, with simultaneous self-organisation and watching over partial interests. The development of these capacities enabled to place imported knowledge and tools into local social context, which is a condition for the successfulness of developmental and catching-up strategies.

The European Union's grand strategies are increasingly important tool for the steering of developmental processes in its Member States. Learning from the relative failure of the Lisbon Strategy, Europe 2020 was much more successful. This is a complex process, in which a nuanced approach to individual countries and the use of contextual intervention and in which mechanisms of Cultural Political Economy can play an important role in ensuring its success.

References

Adam, Frane. 1996. "H. Willke: Kontekstualno usmerjanje. Priložnost za nov razmislek o (Luhmannovi) sistemski teoriji". (H. Willke. Contextual steering: an opportunity for new consideration of (Luhmann's) systems theory). *Teorija in Praksa*, 33(2): 232–247

Adam, Frane and Borut Rončević. 2003. "Social Capital: Recent Debates and Research Trends". *Social Science Information*, 42(2): 155–183.

Adam, Frane, Ivan Bernik and Borut Rončević. 2005. "A Grand Theory and a Small Social Scientific Community: Niklas Luhmann in Slovenia". *Studies in East European Thought*, 57(1): 61–80.

Adam, Frane, Matej Makarovič, Borut Rončević and Matevž Tomšič. 2005. *The Challenges of Sustained Development: The Role of Socio-Cultural Factors in East-Central Europe*. New York; Budapest: Central European University Press.

Alvesson, Mats and André Spicer. 2018. "Neo-Institutional Theory and Organization Studies: A Mid-Life Crisis?" *Organization Studies*, 40(2): 199–218. DOI: https://doi.org/10.1177/0170840618772610

Angelusz, Róbert and Róbert Tardos. 2001. "Change and Stability in Social Network Resources: The Case of Hungary under Transformation". In: Nan Lin, Karen Cook and Ronald S. Burt, eds. *Social Capital: Theory and Research*. New York: Aldine de Gruyter, pp. 297–323.

Archer, Margaret S. 1988. *Culture and Agency*. Cambridge: Cambridge University Press.

Arthur, Brian W. 2021. "Foundations of Complexity Economics". *Nature Reviews Physics*, 3: 136–145. Doi: https://doi.org/10.1038/s42 254-020-00273-3

Banfield, Edward. 1958. *The Moral Basis of a Backward Society*. Glancoe: Free Press.

Beck, Ulrich, Anthony Giddens and Scott Lash. 1994. *Reflexive Modernization: Politics, Tradition and Aesthetics in the Modern Social Order*. Cambridge: Polity.

Bell, Marissa. 2012. "Croatia's Neoliberal Trajectory: The Applicability of Variegated Neoliberalism in the Croatian Postsocialist Context". *Middle States Geographer*, 45: 1–9.

Benton, Richard A., Steve McDonald, Anna Manzoni and David F. Warner. 2015. "The Recruitment Paradox: Network Recruitment, Structural Position, and East German Market Transition". *Social Forces*, 93(3): 905–932.

Berend, Ivan T. 2001. "The Crisis Zone Revisited: Central and Eastern Europe in the 1990s". *East European Politics and Societies*, 15(2): 250–268.

Berend, Ivan T. and György Ránki. 1982. *The European Periphery and Industrialization*. Cambridge: Cambridge University Press.

Berend, Tibor Iván and Bojan Bugarič. 2015. "Unfinished Europe: Transition from Communism to Democracy in Central and Eastern Europe". *Journal of Contemporary History*, 50(4): 768–785.

Bernik, Ivan and Borut Rončević. 2002. "Differenzierte Rezeption der Differezierten Theorie (Zur Rezeption der Luhmannschen Systemtheorie in den Sozialwissenschaften Sloweniens)" (Differentiated Reception of Differentiated Theory (On the Reception of the Luhmann System Theory in the Slovenian Social Sciences)). *Družboslovne Razprave*, 17(37/38): 15–27.

Besednjak Valič, Tamara. 2019. "Innovation, Digitalisation, and the HPC in the Danube Region." In: Borut Rončević, Raluca Coscodaru and Urška Fric, eds. *Go with the Flow: High Performance Computing and Innovations in the Danube Region*. London, Budapest, Ljubljana, pp. 22–46.

Besednjak Valič, Tamara, and Erika Džajić Uršič. 2021. "Addressing Economic Fragmentation: Modelling Regional Gambling Tourism in the Context of Social Fields Theory." *Research in Social Change* 13 (1): 20–36. https://doi.org/10.2478/rsc-2021-0005.

Besednjak Valič, Tamara, and Mirna Macur. 2022. "Meta-analysis of Self-Regulation Discourses in Gambling Through the Sociological Theory of Social Fields." In Janne Nikkinen, Virve Marionneau, and Michael Egerer, eds. *The Global Gambling Industry: Structures, Tactics, and Networks of Impact*. Glücksspielforschung. Wiesbaden: Springer Fachmedien, pp. 87–111. https://doi.org/10.1007/978-3-658-35635-4_7.

Besednjak Valič, Tamara, Janez Kolar, and Urša Lamut. 2020. "Three Scenarios of Innovation and Technology Transfer: The Case of Key Enabling Technologies in the Danube Region." *Journal of Engineering and Applied Sciences* 15: 3619–23.

Besednjak Valič, Tamara, Janez Kolar, and Urša Lamut. 2021. "Fighting the Big Bad Wolf of Global Trends: Technology Transfer between HPC Centres and SMEs." *Digital Policy, Regulation and Governance* ahead-of-print (ahead-of-print). https://doi.org/10.1108/DPRG-11-2020-0162.

Beyer, Jürgen in Jan Wielgohs. 2001. "On the Limits of Path-Dependency Approaches for Explaining Postsocialist Institution Building: In Critical Response to David Stark". *East European Politics and Societies*, 15(2): 356–388.

Borghetto, Enrico and Fabio Franchino. 2010. "The Role of Subnational Authorities in the Implementation of EU Directives". *Journal of European Public Policy*, 17 (6): 759–780.

Bourdieu, Pierre. 1990, 1972. *Outline of a Theory of Practice*. Cambridge: Cambridge University Press.

Bratina, Rok. 2021. "Fight for Media Pluralism or Just 'JanŠA'S War On Media'?" *Research in Social Change* 13 (1): 59–77. https://doi.org/10.2478/rsc-2021-0009.

Brock, William, David A. Hsieh and Blake LeBaron. 1991. *Nonlinear Dynamics, Chaos and Instability*. Cambridge, MA: MIT Press.

Buckley, Walter. 1998. *Society – A Complex Adaptive System: Essays in Social Theory*. Amsterdam: Gordon and Breach Publishers.

Bunce, Valerie. 1998. "Regional Issues in Democratisation: The East Versus the South". *Post-Soviet Affairs*, 14(3): 187–211.

Burawoy, Michael. 2001. "Transition without Transformation: Russia's Involuntary Road to Capitalism". *East European Politics and Societies*, 15(2): 269–290.

Cardoso, Fernando and Enzo Faletto. 1969. *Dependency and Development in Latin America*. Berkeley: California University Press.

Castells, Manuel. 1997. *The Power of Identity. (The Information Age: Economy, Society and Culture: Volume 2)*. Malden; Oxford: Blackwell.

Castells, Manuel. 1998. *End of Millenium (The Information Age: Economy, Society and Culture: Volume 3)*. Malden; Oxford: Blackwell Publishers.

Castilla, Emilio J., Hokyu Hwang, Ellen Granovetter and Mark Granovetter. 2000. "Social Networks in Silicon Valley". In: Chong-Moon Lee, William F. Miller, Marguerite G. Hancock in Henry S. Rowen, eds. *The*

Silicon Valley Edge: A Habitat for Innovation and Entrepreneurship. Stanford: Stanford Business Books, pp. 218–247.

Cepoi, Victor. 2019. "Reshaping the Danube Region Imaginary: A Focus on Digital Transformation and HPC." *Research in Social Change,* 11 (2): 58–78. https://doi.org/10.2478/rsc-2019-0009.

Chandler, Alfred D. 1977. *The Visible Hand – The Managerial Revolution in American Business.* Cambridge, MA: Belknap Press of Harvard University Press.

Corradini, Carlo. 2021. "Local Institutional Quality and Economic Growth: A Panel-VAR Analysis of Italian NUTS-3 Regions." *Economics Letters* 198 (January): 109659. https://doi.org/10.1016/j.econlet.2020.109659

Crozier, Michel. 1970. *Le Société Bloqueé.* Paris: Editions du Seuil.

Cumbers, Andrew, Danny Mackinnon and Keith Chapman. 2003. "Innovation, Collaboration, and Learning in Regional Clusters: A Study of SMEs in the Aberdeen Oil Complex". *Environment and Planning A,* 35(9): 1689–1706.

de Certeau, Michel. 1988. *The Practice of Everyday Life.* Berkeley: University of California Press.

Deutsch, Karl. 1969. *Politische Kybernetik: Modelle und Perspektiven.* Freiburg: Fetscher, Iring.

Drucker, Peter F. 1974. *Management: Tasks, Responsibilities, Practices.* New York: Harper & Row.

Duit, Andreas, Victor Galaz, Katarina Eckerberg and Jonas Ebbesson. 2010. "Governance, Complexity, and Resilience". *Global Environmental Change,* 20(3): 363–368.

Dunford, Michael and Weidong Liu. 2017. "Uneven and Combined Development" *Regional Studies,* 51(1): 69–85, https://doi.org/10.1080/00343404.2016.1262946

Džajić Uršič, Erika. 2019. *Morphogenesis of Industrial Symbiotic Networks.* Berlin: Peter Lang.

Eberlein, Burkard and Dieter Kerwer. 2004. "New Governance in the European Union: A Theoretical Perspective". *Journal of Common Market Studies,* 42(1): 121–142.

Erman, Nuša. 2020. "Prospects for Innovation Performance on European Level." *Research in Social Change* 12 (3): 100–114. https://doi.org/10.2478/rsc-2020-0016.

Esping-Andersen, Gosta. 1996. "Positive-Sum Solutions in a World of Trade-Offs?" In: Gosta Esping-Andersen, ed. *Welfare States in Transition: National Adaptations in Global Economies.* London, Thousand Oaks, New Delhi: Sage, pp. 256–267.

Esser, Klaus, Wolfgang Hillebrand, Dirk Messner in Jörg Meyer Stammer. 1996. *Systemic Competitiveness: New Governance Patterns for Industrial Development.* London: Frank Cass.

Etzioni, Amitai. 1968. *The Active Society. A Theory of Societal and Political Process.* New York: The Free Press.

Evans, Peter. 1997. "Government Action, Social Capital and Development: Reviewing the Evidence on Synergy". In: Peter Evans, ed. *State-Society Synergy: Government and Social Capital in Development.* University of California International and Area Studies Digital Collection, Research Series 94, pp. 178–209. Elsevier Science Ltd.

Fairclough, Norman. 2003. *Analysing Discourse: Textual Analysis for Social Research.* London: Routledge.

Ferran Vila, Susanna, Giorgia Miotto and Josep Rom Rodríguez. 2021. "Cultural Sustainability and the SDGs: Strategies and Priorities in the European Union Countries". *European Journal of Sustainable Development,* 10(2): 73–90. https://doi:10.14207/ejsd.2021.v10n2p73

Foray, Dominique. 2015. *Smart Specialisation: Opportunities and Challenges for Regional Innovation Policy.* Routledge: London and New York.

Fric, Urška. 2019. "Impact of Circular Economy as the EU's Ambitious Policy." *Research in Social Change,* 11 (2): 79–96. https://doi.org/10.2478/rsc-2019-0010.

Gambetta, Diego. 1989. "Mafia: The Price of Distrust". In: Diego Gambetta, ed. *Trust: Making and Breaking Cooperative Relations.* New York: Basil Blackwell Ltd., pp 158–75.

Gangaliuc, Cristian. 2019. "The Measurement of Innovation for Management, Research and Policy." *Research in Social Change,* 11(2): 35–57.

Genov, Nikolai. 1999. *Managing Transformations in Eastern Europe.* Paris: UNESCO-MOST.

Getova, Antoaneta, and Eleonora Mileva. 2021. "Did the Pandemic Permanently Digitalize Higher Education in Bulgaria?" *Research in Social Change*, 13 (1): 191–99. https://doi.org/10.2478/rsc-2021-0019.

Gevorkyan, Aleksandr V. 2018. *Transition Economies: Transformation, Development, and Society in Eastern Europe and the Former Soviet Union*. Oxford: Routledge.

Gibbons, Michael, Camille Limoges, Helga Nowotny, Simon Schwartzman, Peter Scott and Martin Trow. 1996. *The New Production of Knowledge: The Dynamics of Science and Research in Contemporary Societies*. London, Thousand Oaks, New Delhi: Sage Publications.

Giddens, Anthony. 1979. *Central Problem in Sociological Theory*. London: MacMillan.

Giddens, Anthony. 1984. *The Constitution of Society: Outline of the Theory of Structuration*. Cambridge: Polity Press.

Golob, Tea and Matej Makarovič. 2017. "Self-Organisation and Development: A Comparative Approach to Post-communist Transformations from the Perspective of Social Systems Theory". *Europe-Asia studies*, 69(10): 1499–1525.

Golob, Tea and Matej Makarovič. 2021. "Sustainable Development through Morphogenetic Analysis: The Case of Slovenia". *Politics in Central Europe*, 17(1): 83–105.

Golob, Tea, Matej Makarovič and Jana Suklan. 2016. "National Development Generates National Identities". *PloS One*, 11(2): 0146584-1–0146584-14.

Grabher, Gernot and David Stark eds. 2001. *Restrucuring Networks in Eastern Europe*. Oxford: Oxford University Press.

Granovetter, Mark S. 1973. "The Strength of Weak Ties". *American Journal of Sociology*, 78(6): 1360–80.

Granovetter, Mark S. 1985. "Economic Action and Social Structure: The Problem of Embeddedness". *American Journal of Sociology*, 91(3): 481–510.

Gray, Sean W. D. 2020. "Silence and Democratic Institutional Design". *Critical Review of International Social and Political Philosophy*, 24(3): 330–345. https://doi.org/10.1080/13698230.2020.1796331

Greskovits, Bela. 2015. "The Hollowing and Backsliding of Democracy in East Central Europe". *Global Policy*, 6(1): 28–37.

Gudowsky, Niklas and Walter Peissl. 2016. "Human Centred Science and Technology – Transdisciplinary Foresight and Co-creation as Tools for Active Needs-based Innovation Governance". *European Journal of Futures Research*, 4(8), article 8. https://doi.org/10.1007/s40 309-016-0090-4.

Haček, Miro, Simona Kukovič and Marjan Brezovšek. 2013. "Problems of Corruption and Distrust in Political and Administrative Institutions in Slovenia". *Communist and Post-communist Studies*, 46(2): 255–261.

Hafner, Ana and Dolores Modic. 2020. "European Automotive Technological Innovation Systems in the Age of Disruption: The Suppliers' View." *Research in Social Change*, 12 (3): 53–77. https://doi.org/10.2478/rsc-2020-0014.

Haverland, Markus and Marleen Romeijn. 2007. "Do Member States Make European Policies Work? Analysing the EU Transposition Deficit." *Public Administration*, 85(3): 757–78.

Held, David. 1991. "Democracy, the Nation State and the Global System". *Economy and Society*, 20(2): 138–172.

Helmig, Jan and Oliver Kessler. 2007. "Space, Boundaries, and the Problem of Order: A View from Systems Theory". *International Political Sociology*, 1(3): 240–256. doi:10.1111/j.1749-5687.2007.00016.x.

Helmut, Willke. 2009. *Governance in a Disenchanted World: The End of Moral Society*. Cheltenham and Northampton: Edward Elgar Publishing.

Hendry, John in David Seidl. 2002. "The Structure and Significance of Strategic Episodes Soocial Systems Theory and the Routine Practices of Strategic Change". Paper presented at European Academy of management, 9–11 May 2002 in Stockholm.

Hessels, Laurens K. and Harro van Lente. 2008. "Re-thinking New Knowledge Production: A Literature Review and a Research Agenda". *Research Policy*, 37: 740–760. doi:10.1016/j.respol.2008.01.008.

Heylighen, Francis. 1992. "Principles of Systems and Cybernetics: an Evolutionary Perspective" In: Robert Trappl, ed. *Cybernetics and Systems* '92. Singapore: World Science, pp. 3–10.

Hirst, Paul, Grahame Thompson and Simon Bromley. 2009. *Globalization in Question*, 3rd edition. Cambridge: Polity Press.

Janos, Andrew C. 2001. "From Eastern Empire to Western Hegemony: East Central Europe under Two International Regimes". *East European Politics and Societies*, 15(2): 221–249.

Jessop, Bob. 2004. "Critical Semiotic Analysis and Cultural Political Economy." *Critical Discourse Studies*, 1(2): 159–174.

Jessop, Bob. 2008. *State Power: A Strategic-Relational Approach.* Cambridge: Polity Press.

Jessop, Bob. 2010. "Cultural Political Economy and Critical Policy Studies." *Critical Policy Studies*, 3(3–4): 336–356.

Jessop, Bob and Stijn Oosterlynck. 2008. "Cultural Political Economy: On Making the Cultural Turn without Falling into Soft Economic Sociology." *Geoforum*, 39(3): 1155–1169.

Kaplinsky, Raphael and Dirk Messner. 2008. "Introduction: The Impact of Asian Drivers on the Developing World". *World Development*, 36(2): 197–209.

Karl, Terry L. and Philippe C. Scmitter. 1995. "From an Iron Curtain to a Paper Curtain: Grounding Transitologists or Students of Postcommunism". *Slavic Review*, 54(4): 965–978.

Kasprzyk, Beata and Jolanta Wojnar. 2021. "An Evaluation of the Implementation of the Europe 2020 Strategy". *Economic and Regional Studies / Studia Ekonomiczne i Regionalne*, 14(2): 146–157.

Katzenstein, Peter J. 1985. *Small States in World Markets: Industrial Policy in Europe*. Ithaca: Cornell University Press.

Kenis, Patrick and Volker Schneider. 1991. "Policy Networks and Policy Analysis: Scrutinising a New Analytical Toolbox". In: Bernd Marin and Renate Mayntz, eds. *Policy Network: Empirical Evidence and Theoretical Considerations*. Frankfurt am Main: Campus Verlag, pp. 25–59.

Kessler, Oliver and Jan Helmig. 2007. "Of Systems, Boundaries, and Regionalisation". *Geopolitics*, 12(4), 570–585. doi: https://10.1080/14650040701546053

Kim, Linsu and Richard R. Nelson, eds. 2000. *Technology, Learning, and Innovation: Experiences of Newly Industrializing Economies*. Cambridge: Cambridge University Press.

Kleindienst, Petra. 2017. "Understanding the Different Dimensions of Human Dignity: Analysis of the Decision of the Constitutional Court of the Republic of Slovenia on the "Tito street" Case." *Danube: Law and Economics Review,* 8(3): 117–147, DOI: 10.1515/danb-2017-0009.

Kleindienst, Petra. 2019. "Zgodovinski temelji sodobne paradigme človekovega dostojanstva." (The historical foundations of the modern paradigm of human dignity.) *Phainomena,* 28(108/109): 259–282, DOI: 10.32022/PHI28.2019.108-109.11.

Kleindienst, Petra. 2019a. "Pomen človekovega dostojanstva v delih Giovannija Pica della Mirandola." (The importance of human dignity in the works of Giovanni Pico della Mirandola). *Ars & Humanitas,* 13(1): 285–301, DOI: 10.4312/ars.13.1.285-301.

Kleindienst, Petra and Matevž Tomšič. 2017. "Human Dignity as the Foundation of Democratic Political Culture: Legal and Philosophical Perspective." *Law, Culture and the Humanities,* 1–20. Doi: 10.1177 / 1743872117738229.

Kleindienst, Petra and Matevž Tomšič. 2018. "Human Dignity as an Element of Political Culture in the New Democracies: The Case of the Post-Communist Slovenia." *Bogoslovni vestnik-Theological quarterly-Ephemerides Theologicae,* 78 (1): 159–70.

Kleindienst, Petra and Matevž Tomšič. 2021. "Proces narodne sprave in vloga politične elite v njem: Slovenija kot izjema med državami srednje in vzhodne Evrope." (The process of national reconciliation and the role of the political elite in it: Slovenia as an exception between the countries of Central and Eastern Europe.) *Studia Historica Slovenica: časopis za humanistične in družboslovne študije,* 21 (1): 197–232, DOI: 10.32874/SHS.2021-07.

Kouwenhoven, Vincent. 1993. "The Rise of the Public Private Partnership: A Model for the Management of Public–Private Cooperation". In: Jan Kooiman, ed. *Modern Governance: New Government–Society Interactions.* Sage: London, pp. 119–130.

Kukovič, Simona. 2022. "How Novel Coronavirus Has Shaken Public Trust in Decision-Making Institutions: Comparative Analysis of Selected European Union Members". *Journal of Comparative Politics,* 15(1): 9–19.

Labianca Giuseppe and Daniel J. Brass. 2006. "Exploring the Social Ledger: Negative Relationships and Negative Asymmetry in Social Networks in Organizations". *Academy of Management Review,* 31(3): 596–614.

Landes, David S. 1998. *The Wealth and Poverty of Nations: Why Some Are So Rich and Some So Poor.* New York: W.W. Norton & Company.

Leydesdorff, Loet. 2010. "Luhmann Reconsidered: Steps Towards an Empirical Research Program in the Sociology of Communication". In: Colin B. Grant, ed. *Beyond Universal Pragmatics: Essays in the Philosophy of Communication.* Oxford: Peter Lang, pp. 149–173.

Lindblom, Charles E. 1959. "The Science of 'muddling through'". *Public Administration Review,* 19(2): 79–88.

Luhmann, Niklas. 1995, 1984. *Social Systems.* Stanford: Stanford University Press.

Ma, Shu-Yun. 1998. "Third World Studies, Development Studies and Post-Communist Studies: Definitions, Distance and Dynamism". *Third World Quarterly,* 19(3): 339–348.

Macur, Mirna. 2021. "The Impact of Digitalisation on Slovenian Primary School Students in Eighth Grade." *Research in Social Change* 13 (1): 174–80. https://doi.org/10.2478/rsc-2021-0017.

Majetić, Filip, Matej Makarovič, Dražen Šimleša and Tea Golob. 2019. "Performance of Work Integration Social Enterprises in Croatia, Slovenia, and Italian Regions of Lombardy and Trentino". *Economics & sociology.* 12(1): 286–301.

Makarovič, Matej. 2001. *Usmerjanje modernih družb.* (Steering contemporary societies.) Ljubljana: Znanstveno in publicistično središče.

Makarovič, Matej and Mateja Rek. 2017. "Experts and the Macro Level Decision-Making in the Information Society". In: Borut Rončević and Matevž Tomšič, eds. *Information Society and Its Manifestations: Economy, Politics, Culture.* Frankfurt am Main: Peter Lang.

Makarovič, Matej, Janez Šušteršič and Borut Rončević. 2014. "Is Europe 2020 se to fail? The Cultural Political Economy of the EU Grand Strategies." *European Planning Studies,* 22 (3): 610–626.

Mayntz, Renate. 1993. "Policy-Netzwerke und die Logik der Verhandlungssystemen". In: Adrianne Héritier, ed. *Policy-Analyse: Kritik und Neuorientierung.* Opladen: Westdeutscher Verlag, pp. 39–56.

Mayntz, Renate. 2016. "Steering". In: Ansell Christopher and Jacob Torling, eds. *Handbook on Theories of Governance.* Cheltenham: Edward Elgar Publishing Limited, pp. 278–284.

Mayntz, Renate and Eberhard Bohne. 1978. *Vollzugsprobleme der Umweltpolitik: Empirische Untersuchung der Implementation von Gesetzen im Bereich der Luftreinhaltung und des Gewässerschutzes.* (Enforcement problems of environmental policy: Empirical study of the implementation of laws in the field of air pollution control and water protection.) Stuttgart: Kohlhammer.

McNally, Christopher A. 2019. "Chaotic mélange: Neo-liberalism and Neo-statism in the Age of Sino-capitalism". *Review of International Political Economy,* 27(2): 1–21. https://10.1080/09692290.2019.1683595

Meijerink, Gerdien. 2011. "New Institutional Economics: Douglass North and Masahiko Aoki." In: Sietze Vellema, ed. *Transformation and Sustainability in Agriculture.* Wageningen: Wageningen Academic Publishers, pp. 21–33. https://doi.org/10.3920/978-90-8686-717-2_2.

Messner, Dirk. 2013. *The Network Society: Economic Development and International Competitiveness as Problems of Social Governance.* Abington: Routledge.

Mintzberg, Henry. 1989. *Mintzberg on Management: Inside Our Strange World of Organizations.* New York: The Free Press.

Mintzberg, Henry. 1998. "The Strategy Concept I: Five Ps for Strategy". In: Harry Costin, ed. *Readings in Strategy and Strategic Planning.* Fort Worth: The Dryden Press, pp. 33–44.

Modic, Dolores and Borut Rončević. 2018. "Social Topography for Sustainable Innovation Policy: Putting Institutions, Social Networks and Cognitive Frames in Their Place". *Comparative Sociology,* 17(1): 100–127.

Modic, Dolores, Ana Hafner, and Tamara Valič-Besednjak. 2022. "Every Woman Is a Vessel: An Exploratory Study on Gender and Academic Entrepreneurship in a Nascent Technology Transfer System." In: Joaquín M. Azagra-Caro, Pablo D'Este, and David Barberá-Tomás, eds. *University-Industry Knowledge Interactions: People, Tensions and Impact.* International Studies in Entrepreneurship. Cham: Springer International Publishing, pp. 159–78. https://doi.org/10.1007/978-3-030-84669-5_9.

Mugarura, Jude Thaddeo, Zwelinzima Ndevu and Peter Turyakira. 2020. "Unleashing Public Private Partnership Understanding and the Ideal Underpinning Theories: A Public Sector View". *Public Administration Research,* 9(1): 14–29.

Nee, Victor. 1998. "Sources of New Institutionalism". In: Mary C. Brinton and Victor Nee, eds. *The New Institutionalism in Sociology.* Stanford: Stanford University Press, pp. 1–16.

Nee, Victor and Mary C. Brinton. 1998. "Introduction". In: Mary C. Brinton and Victor Nee, eds. *The New Institutionalism in Sociology.* Stanford: Stanford University Press, pp. xv–xix.

Nielsen, Klaus, Bob Jessop and Jerzy Hausner. 1995. "Institutional Change in Post-Socialism". In: Jerzy Hausner, Bob Jessop and Klaus Nielsen, eds. *Strategic Choice and Path-Dependency in Post-Socialism: Institutional Dynamics in the Transformation Process.* Aldershot: Edward Elgar, pp. 3–44.

Nieto, Maria Jesus and Santamaria Lluis. 2007. "The Importance of Diverse Collaborative Networks for the Novelty of Product Innovation". *Technovation,* 27(6–7): 367–377. DOI: 10.1016/j.technovation.2006.10.001.

North, Douglass C. 1990. *Institutions, Institutional Change and Economic Performance.* Cambridge: Cambridge University Press.

North, Douglass C. 2010. *Understanding the Process of Economic Change.* The Princeton Economic History of the Western World. Princeton: Princeton University Press.

Nozick, Robert. 1974. *Anarchy, State and Utopia.* New York: Basic Books.

Offe, Claus. 1995. "Institutional Design, Strategic Dilemmas, and the Dynamics of Post-Socalist Transformation". In: Jerzy Hausner, Bob Jessop in Klaus Nielsen, eds. *Strategic Choice and Path-Dependency in Post-Socialism: Institutional Dynamics in the Transformation Process.* Aldershot: Edward Elgar, pp. 47–66.

O'Hearn, Dennis. 1998. *Inside the Celtic Tiger: The Irish Economy and the Asian Model.* Dublin: Pluto.

Ormerod, Paul. 1994. *The Death of Economics.* London: Faber & Faber.

Ostrom, Elinor. 1997. "Crossing the Great Divide: Coproduction, Synergy and Development". In: Peter Evans, ed. *State-Society Synergy: Government and Social Capital in Development.* University of California International and Area Studies Digital Collection, Research Series 94, pp. 85–118.

Ostrom, Elinor. 1999. "Institutional Rational Choice: An Assessment of the Institutional Analysis and Development Framework". In: Paul

Sabatier, ed. *Theories of the Policy Process*. Boulder: Westview Press, pp. 35–71.

Pandiloska Jurak, Alenka. 2019. "Public Policy Instrument Evaluation in Service of Enabling Grand Strategy Discourse – Case of Horizon 2020 Key Indicators." *Research in Social Change,* 11 (2): 97–121. https://doi.org/10.2478/rsc-2019-0011.

Pandiloska Jurak, Alenka. 2020. "The Importance of High – Tech Companies for EU Economy – Overview and the EU Grand Strategies Perspective." *Research in Social Change,* 12 (3): 32–52. https://doi.org/10.2478/rsc-2020-0013.

Pandiloska Jurak, Alenka. 2021. "The Role of Social Capital for Slovenian High-Tech Companies' Internationalization." *Research in Social Change* 13 (1): 111–19. https://doi.org/10.2478/rsc-2021-0012.

Pillai, Kishore Gopalakrishna, Gerard P. Hodgkinson, Gurumurthy Kalyanaram and Smitha R. Nair. 2015. "The Negative Effects of Social Capital in Organizations: A Review and Extension". *International Journal of Management Reviews,* 19(1): 97–124. DOI: 10.1111/ijmr.12085.

Polany, Karl. 2001, 1944. *The Great Transformation: The Political and Economic Origins of Our Time*. Boston: Beacon Press.

Polk, Merritt. 2015. "Transdisciplinary Co-production: Designing and Testing a Transdisciplinary Research Framework for Societal Problem Solving". *Futures,* 62(Special Issue): 110–122. doi: 10.1016/j.futures.2014.11.001.

Porter, Michael. 1980. *Competitive Strategy. Techniques for Analysing Industries and Competitors*. New York: The Free Press.

Porter, Michael. 1990. *The Competitive Advantage of Nations*. New York: The Free Press.

Portes, Alejandro. 1998. "Social Capital: Its Origins and Applications in Modern Sociology." *Annual review of Sociology,* 24: 1–24.

Poznanski, Kazimierz Z. 2001. "Building Capitalism with Communist Tools: Eastern Europe's Defective Transition." *East European Politics and Societies,* 15(2): 320–355.

Prijon, Lea, and Matevž Tomšič. 2021. "Elite Profile and Type of Institutional Transformation: Comparison of Russia and Slovenia." *Research in Social Change* 13 (1): 129–39. https://doi.org/10.2478/rsc-2021-0014.

Ranchod, Rushi and Christopher Vas. 2019. "Policy Networks Revisited: Creating a Researcher-Policymaker Community". *Evidence & Policy*, 15(1): 31–47. DOI: 10.1332/174426417X15139342679329.

Rek, Mateja, Matej Makarovič and Matjaž Škabar. 2017. "Identifying Complex Cultural Conditions of Globalization in Late Modernity: A Fuzzy Set Analysis of 30 Countries". *European Journal of Science and Theology*, 13(1): 173–188.

Ritzer, George and Douglas J. Goodman. 2003. *Sociological Theory*. Boston: McGraw Hill.

Rolland, Knut-H., and Ole Hanseth. 2021. "Managing Path Dependency in Digital Transformation Processes: A Longitudinal Case Study of an Enterprise Document Management Platform." *Procedia Computer Science* 181: 765–74. https://doi.org/10.1016/j.procs.2021.01.229

Rončević, Borut. 2002. "Participatory Policy Process in Southeast Europe". In: Irina Kausch and Alfred Pfaller, eds. *Employment and Labour-Market Policy in South Eastern Europe*. Belgrad: Friedrich Ebert Stiftung, pp. 205–211.

Rončević, Borut. 2019. "Cultural Political Economy of Europe 2020: Jean Monnet Chair CPE 2020 and Its Impact." *Research in Social Change,* 11(2): 5–13. https://doi.org/10.2478/rsc-2019-0006.

Rončević, Borut. 2020. "Technology and Innovations in Regional Development for Europe 2020: Jean Monnet Centre of Excellence TIR 2020 for Smart, Inclusive and Sustainable Growth." *Research in Social Change* 12(3): 5–14. https://doi.org/10.2478/rsc-2020-0011.

Rončević, Borut and Dolores Modic. 2011. "Regional Systems of Innovations as Social Fields". *Sociologija i prostor: časopis za istraživanje prostornog i sociokulturnog razvoja*, 49(191): 313–333.

Rončević, Borut and Matej Makarovič. 2010. "Towards the Strategies of Modern Societies: Systems and Social Processes." *Innovation – The European Journal of Social Science Research,* 23(3): 223–239.

Rončević, Borut, Dolores Modic and Tea Golob. 2022. "Social-Fields-Approach (SOFIA) to Research on Social Change: Innovations as Social Fields". In: Borut Rončević and Victor Cepoi, eds. *Technologies and Innovations in Regional Development: The European Union and Its Strategies*. Berlin: Peter Lang, pp. 9–28.

Rostow, Walt. 1960. *The Stages of Economic Growth: A Non-communist Manifesto.* Cambridge: Cambridge University Press.

Saunila, Minna. 2017. "Understanding Innovation Performance Measurement in SMEs." *Measuring Business Excellence,* 21(1): 1–16.

Scharpf, Fritz. 1972. "Komplexität als Schranke der Politischen Planung". (Complexty as spaces for political planning.) *Politische Vierteljahrschriften,* 4: 168–192.

Scharpf, Fritz. 1993. "Positive und Negative Koordination in Verhandlungssystemen". (Positive and negative coordination in negotiation systems.) In: Adrianne Héritier, ed. *Policy-Analyse.* Opladen: Westdeutcher Verlag, pp. 57–83.

Schrank, Andrew and Josh Whitford. 2011. "The Anatomy of Network Failure". *Sociological Theory,* 29(3): 151–177. doi: 10.1111/ j.1467-9558.2011.01392.x.

Schumpeter, Joseph A. 1934. *The Theory of Economic Development.* Cambrigde, MA: Harvard University Press.

Scmitter, Philippe C. 1979. "Still the Century of Corporatism?" In: Philippe C. Schmitter and Gerhard Lehmbruch, eds. *Trends Towards Corporatist Intermediation.* London and Beverly Hills: Sage, pp. 7–52.

Seidl, David. 2003. "The Role of General Strategy Concepts in the Practice of Strategy". Paper presented at 19th EGOS colloquium in Copenhagen, 3–5 July 2003.

Seidl, David and Hannah Mormann (2015). "Niklas Luhmann as Organization Theorist". In Paul Adler, Paul du Gay, Glenn Morgan and Mike Reed, eds. *Oxford Handbook of Sociology, Social Theory and Organization Studies: Contemporary Currents.* Oxford: Oxford University Press, pp. 125–157.

Selznick, Philip. 1957. *Leadership in Administration: A Sociological Interpretation.* New York: Harper & Row.

Shahab, Sina, and Leonhard K. Lades. 2021. "Sludge and Transaction Costs." *Behavioural Public Policy,* April, 1–22. https://doi.org/10.1017/ bpp.2021.12.

Shleifer, Andrei and Daniel Treisman. 2014. "Normal Countries: The East 25 Years After Communism." *Foreign Affairs,* 93(6): 92–103. *JSTOR,* www.jstor.org/stable/24483924.

Singh, Swapnil, and Guru Ashish Singh. 2021. "Assessing the Impact of the Digital Divide on Indian Society: A Study of Social Exclusion." *Research in Social Change* 13 (1): 181–90. https://doi.org/10.2478/rsc-2021-0018.

Skivko, Maria. 2021. "Digital Technologies, Social Entrepreneurship and Governance for Sustainable Development." *Research in Social Change* 13 (1): 165–73. https://doi.org/10.2478/rsc-2021-0016.

So, Alvin Y. 1990. *Social Change and Development: Modernization, Dependency and World-System Theories*. London: Sage.

Sorge, Arndt. 1996. "Societal Effects in Cross-National Organization Studies: Conceptualising Diversity in Actors and Systems". In: Richard Whitley and Peer Hull Kristensen, eds. *The Changing European Firm: Limits to Convergence*. London in New York: Routledge, pp. 67–86.

Stacey, Ralph. 1996. *Complexity and Creativity in Organisations*. San Francisco: Berret-Koehler.

Stark, David. 1995. "Not by Design: The Myth of Designer Capitalism in Eastern Europe". In: Jerzy Hausner, Bob Jessop and Klaus Nielsen, eds. *Strategic Choice and Path-Dependency in Post-Socialism: Institutional Dynamics in the Transformation Process*. Aldershot: Edward Elgar, pp. 67–83.

Stec, Małgorzata and Mariola Grzebyk (2018). "The Implementation of the Strategy Europe 2020 Objectives in European Union Countries: The Concept Analysis and Statistical Evaluation" *Quality and Quantity*, 52: 119. https://doi.org/10.1007/s11135-016-0454-7

Stephenson, Paul. 2013. "Twenty Years of Multi-level Governance: 'Where Does It Come From? What Is It? Where Is It Going?'". *Journal of European Public Policy*, 20(6): 817–837, DOI: 10.1080/13501763.2013.781818.

Šubrt, Jiří. 2020. *The Systematic Approach in Sociology and Niklas Luhmann: Expectations, Discussions, Doubts*. Bingley: Emerald.

Sum, Ngai-Ling and Bob Jessop. 2014. Toward a Cultural Political Economy: Putting Culture in Its Place in Political Economy. *Edward Elgar: Cheltenham, UK and Northampton, USA*.

Szelenyi, Ivan. 2014. "Pathways from and Crises after Communism: the Case of Central Eastern Europe". *Belvedere Meridionale*, 26(4): 7–23.

Sztompka, Piotr. 1993. *The Sociology of Social Change*. Oxford: Blackwell.

Szymańska, Agata. 2021. "Reducing Socioeconomic Inequalities in the European Union in the Context of the 2030 Agenda for Sustainable Development". *Sustainability*, 13(13): 7409. https://doi.org/10.3390/su13137409

Thompson, J.D. 1967. *Organizations in Action*. New York: McGraw-Hill.

Tomšič, Matevž and Urban Vehovar. 2012. "Quality of Governance in "old" and "new" EU Member States in a Comparative Perspective." *Sociologia*, 44(3): 367–384.

Torfing, Jacob. 2001. "Path-Dependent Danish Welfare Reforms: The Contribution of the New Institutionalisms to Understanding Evolutionary Change". *Scandinavian Political Studies*, 24(4): 277–309.

Torsvik, Gaute. 2000. "Social Capital and Economic Development: A Plea for the Mechanisms". *Rationality and Society*, 12: 451–476.

Tutak Magdalena, Jarosław Brodny and Peter Bindzár. 2021. "Assessing the Level of Energy and Climate Sustainability in the European Union Countries in the Context of the European Green Deal Strategy and Agenda 2030". *Energies*, 14(6): 1767. https://doi.org/10.3390/en14061767

Uršič, Erika D. 2020. "Systematized Analysis Using Data Mining's Methodology on the Topic of Regional Industrial Symbiosis and Its Networks". *Research in Social Change*, 12(3): 78–99.

van Assche, Kristoph, Martijn Duineveld, Gert Verschraegen, Roel During and Raoul Beunen. 2011. "Social Systems and Social Engineering: Niklas Luhmann". In: Sietze Vellema, ed. *Transformation and Sustainability in Agriculture: Connecting Practice with Social Theory*. Wageningen: Wageningen Academic Publishers, pp. 35–48.

van Hemert, Patricia, Peter Nijkamp and Jolanda Verbraak. 2009. "Evaluating Social Science and Humanities Knowledge Production: An Exploratory Analysis of Dynamics in Science Systems". *Innovation: The European Journal of Social Science Research*, 22(4): 443–464. DOI:10.1080/13511610903457589.

Vasileiadou, Eleftheria and Karolina Safarzynska. 2010. "Transitions: Taking Complexity Seriously". *Futures*, 42(10): 1176–1186. DOI: https://10.1016/j.futures.2010.07.001

Walker, Gordon, Bruce Kogut and Weijian Shan. 1997. "Social Capital, Structural Holes and the Formation of an Industry Network." *Organization Science*, 8(2): 109–125.

Wanzenböck, Iris and Koen Frenken. 2020. "The Subsidiarity Principle in Innovation Policy for Societal Challenges". *Global Transitions*, 2: 51–59. https://doi.org/10.1016/j.glt.2020.02.002

Weber, Max. 2002. *Protestantska etika in duh kapitalizma.* (Protestant ethics and the spirit of capitalism.) Ljubljana: Studia Humanitatis.

Weiss, Linda. 1998. *The Myth of the Powerless State*. Ithaca: Cornell University Press.

Weiss, Linda and John M. Hobson. 1995. *States and Economic Development*. Cambridge: Polity Press.

Westlund, Hans and Frane Adam. 2010. "Social Capital and Economic Performance: A Meta-analysis of 65 Studies". *European Planning Studies*, 18(6): 893–919.

Whitley, Richard ed. 1992. *European Business Systems: Firms and Markets in Their National Contexts*. London: Sage.

Whitley, Richard. 1996. "The Social Construction of Economic Actors. Institutions and Types of Firm in Europe and Other Market Economies". In: Richard Whitley and Peer Hull Kristensen, eds. *The Changing European Firm: Limits to Convergence*. London and New York: Routledge, pp. 39–66.

Whittam, Geoff and Mike Danson. 2001. "Power and the Spirit of Clustering". *European Planning Studies*, 9(8): 949–963.

Whittington, Richard. 1993. *What Is Strategy – and Does It Matter*. London: Routledge.

Whittington, Richard. 2002. "The Work of Strategizing and Organizing: For a Practice Perspective". *Strategic Organization*, 1(1): 119–127.

Wiarda, Howard. 2002. "Southern Europe, Eastern Europe, and Comparative Politics: 'Transitology' and The Need for New Theory". *East European Politics and Society*, 15(3): 485–501.

Williams, Teshanee, Jamie McCall, Maureen Berner and Anita Brown-Graham. 2021. "Beyond Bridging and Bonding: The Role of Social Capital in Organizations". *Community Development Journal*, bsab025, https://doi.org/10.1093/cdj/bsab025

Williamson, Oliver E. 1975. *Markets and Hierarcies*. New York: Free Press.

Williamson, Oliver E. 1991. "The Logic of Economic Organization". In: Oliver E. Williamson and Sidney G. Winter, eds. *The Nature of the Firm – Origins, Evolution, and Development*. Oxford: Oxford University Press, pp. 90–116.

Williamson, Oliver E. 1993. "Calculativeness, Trust, and Economic Organization." *The Journal of Law and Economics* 36 (1, Part 2): 453–86. https://doi.org/10.1086/467284.

Willke, Helmut. 1992. *Ironie des Staates*. (Irony of the State.) Frankfurt am Main: Suhrkamp.

Willke, Helmut. 1993. *Sistemska teorija razvitih družb: dinamika in tveganost moderne družbene samoorganizacije*. (Systems theory of developed societies: dynamics and risk of modern social self-organization.) Ljubljana: Fakulteta za družbene vede.

Willke, Helmut. 1993a. *Systemtheorie*. (Systems Theory.) Stuttgart: Gustav Fischer Verlag.

Willke, Helmut. 2009. *Governance in a Disenchanted World. The End of Moral Society*. Cheltenham and Northampton: Edward Elgar.

Wrong, Dennis. 1961. "The Oversocialised Conception of Man in Modern Sociology". *American Sociological Review*, 26: 183–193.

Wüst, Charlotte and Nicky Rogge. 2022. "How Is the European Union Progressing towards Its Europe 2020 Targets? A Benefit-of-the-Doubt Window Analysis." *Empirica*, 49: 405–438.

Zeleny, Milan. 1997. "Autopoieis and Self-Sustainability in Economic Systems". *Human Systems Management*, 16: 251–262.

Zeleny, Milan. 2001. "Autopoiesis (Self-production) in SME Networks". *Human Systems Management*, 20(3): 201–207.

Zeng, S.X., X.M. Xie and C.M. Tam. 2010. "Relationship between Cooperation Networks and Innovation Performance of SMEs". *Technovation*, 30(3): 181–194. doi: 10.1016/j.technovation.2009.08.003.

Zdravje, Peter. 2021. "Co-Governance, Social Responsibility and Economic Democracy." *Research in Social Change* 13 (1): 140–49. https://doi.org/10.2478/rsc-2021-0015.

Index

Printed by
CPI books GmbH, Leck